Sheet Metal Fabrication Basics

Rob Roehl/Timothy Remus

Published by:
Wolfgang Publications Inc.
PO Box 223
Stillwater, MN 55082
www.wolfpub.com

Legals

First published in 2007 by Wolfgang Publications Inc.,
PO Box 223, Stillwater MN 55082

© Timothy Remus, 2007

The information in this book is true and complete to the best of our
knowledge. All recommendations are made without any guarantee
on the part of the author or publisher, who also disclaim any liability
incurred in connection with the use of this data or specific details.

We recognize that some words, model names and designations, for
example, mentioned herein are the property of the trademark holder.
We use them for identification purposes only. This is not an official
publication.

ISBN number: 1-929133-46-4

Printed and bound in China

Sheet Metal Fabrication Basics

Acknowledgements

This book grew out of conversations with Rob Roehl regarding the need for a very basic metal fabrication book. Rob was quick to say, "people get intimidated by the tools they think they need, but you really don't need much to get started." Thus was born the idea of co-authoring a book that emphasized the methods and theory, and not the fancy power tools.

The projects Rob chose to include in this book are very typical of the sheet metal fabrication projects that come through any custom bike-building shop. Most of these are real projects, that is, work Rob had to perform, whether I was there with the camera or not. Which brings up the next person to thank and that would be Donnie Smith, who made it possible for Rob to take extra time for these fabrication projects so I could take photos.

Next on the list are two "guest editors," Bruce Terry and Ron Covell. If the name Bruce Terry isn't as familiar as that of Ron Covell, it's because Bruce spends most of his time working away quietly on rare and exotic automobiles. Most of these jobs require that Bruce reproduce a fender or more for an old Jaguar or Rolls Royce, to create a part that is no longer available. For Bruce, the chance to build a fender from scratch meant creative freedom, and an opportunity to make the fender to his dimensions, not some one else's.

Guest editor number two is the well-known fabricator Ron Covell. Ron once again shared his skills and good humor with me for the better part of two days while he make an air dam for a chopper frame. To make things more interesting Ron built the part from aluminum and then did nearly half of the welding with a gas-welding outfit.

Welding is an essential part of fabricating and for help in this department I called local street rod fabricators Kurt Senescall and Pat Kary. Kurt answered my questions on welding and sheet metal fabrication in general while Pat did a variety of welding demonstrations using both TIG and oxy-acetylene. A new TIG welding setup might be nice, but it ain't essential.

Assembling the book and processing hundreds of photos is the work of our two graphic designers, Jacki Mitchell and Deb Shade. To pay the printer and help run the office we all rely on Krista Leary. Final proof reading is the domain of my lovely and talented wife Mary Lanz. To one and all I tip my hat.

Timothy Remus

Introduction

I like to say, "if you want to learn something, ask the person who does it all day, day after day, and takes great pride in that work." In the case of this Sheet Metal Fabrication book, I found five metal fabricators willing to show all of us how it is they make such beautiful shapes from flat sheet steel and aluminum.

Though the lessons presented here could easily be applied to cars or airplanes, the projects themselves are pure motorcycle: How to mount a fender, Fabricate a set of pipes, Add tails to a gas tank, Fabricate an air dam, or Make a fender from scratch.

Author Rob Roehl leans over one of his hand-fabricated motorcycle projects.

The idea is to present projects and methods that anyone with some basic tools and the raw desire can create in a small shop – without a lot or expensive equipment. As Rob Roehl explains. "All you really need to do this work is some hammers, a bag of sand and maybe a small shrinker. You don't have to have a power hammer or an English wheel."

So before you run out and spend a thousand dollars or more on equipment, take a look at all the projects that populate the pages of this book. The only "power tool" you'll see is a band saw and some limited use of an English wheel. What you will see are a number of experienced and talented individuals making useful shapes from raw stock with only the most basic of tools, including rubber mallets and even a hollowed out tree stump.

A good how-to book should be like walking into the shop of an expert for a one-on-one lesson. To add to that sensation the fabricators in this book wrote their own captions – so the explanations are their own and the lessons more genuine.

In addition to a series of fabricating sequences we've presented a separate chapter on welding both steel and aluminum with either TIG or oxy-acetylene. Again, it's not the size of your toolbox that makes you a good or bad fabricator – it's the size of your determination.

Chapter One

Planning & Design

If It Looks Right, It Is Right

When I do planning, the biggest thing is the customer, what does he or she want for style. I try to get a good feel for whatever he or she wants to do. You need a mental plan, I ask myself, 'where do I want to end up.'

The budget is a big part of this. Will the bike use tanks built from scratch or should I use blanks to fabricate the tanks, or just modify an existing tank.

Then, if I'm doing a one-off tank, I think

At the Donnie Smith Custom Cycles shop, they sometimes use light poster board as shown here to help in the design process. The idea for Donnie's 300 tire Bagger is to make it look cool and modern without completely loosing the signature look of a "Bagger."

about the style of the tank, what shape of tank do I want and do I want to embellish it. Does it need to have a certain capacity. If it's a little bar hopper then the capacity doesn't matter. A lot of this goes along with the wants and desires of the customer and how the bike will be used.

Planning also means getting the initial style and direction and sticking with it. I tell people to 'try to start right and stay right.' You need to be fluid as you go along, but still stay with the theme so it doesn't end up being three motorcycles.'

After I get the initial plan, I might do cardboard mock-ups and profiles.

BE FLEXIBLE, TO A POINT

Once I get into the fabrication process and can set parts on the bike I may decide the tank needs more or less arch.

Sometimes I do sketches, but if I do it's just a quick sketch. Donnie and I understand each other so when we're working on a project we generally don't need a sketch. And I don't do bucks at all. If I was going to make more than one I would consider the bucks, but I never make the same thing twice.

For the gas tank Rob and Donnie cut out a variety of shapes before deciding on this one. The beauty of the poster board is the ease with which a new shape can be tested. Though it's more work, you can also buy foam and cut it into various three-dimensional shapes.

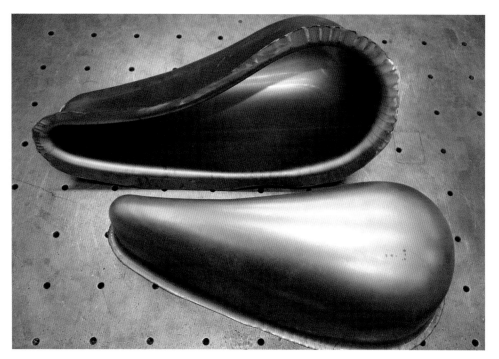

Making a gas tank is a tremendous amount of work so Rob decided in this case to use stamped Fat Katz tank blanks from D&D. "They have the shape that Donnie wants," explains Rob, "and are a big time saver for me."

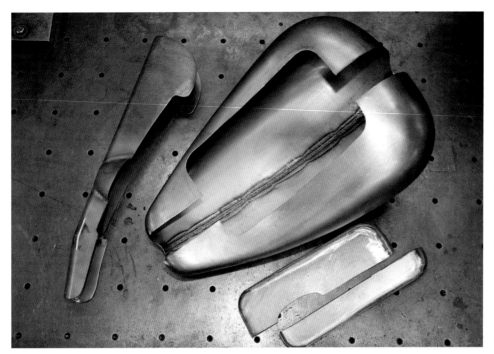

"To make the tank I cut off the flanges and welded the two halves together. Then I cut the bottom out for the tunnel."

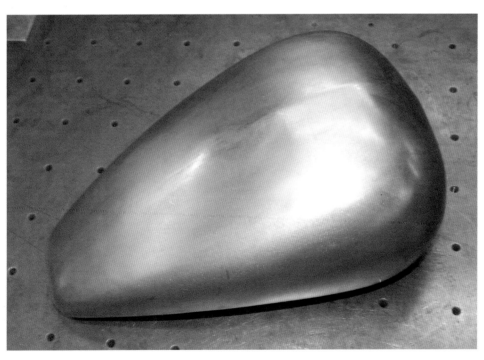

The nearly finished tank, though the story has one more interesting wrinkle.

When I start on a tank I get a bottom profile first, the bottom has to be where it has to be. And then I begin the shaping part of the process. I want the tank as wide or wider than the forks. Then I make a basic shape and set it on the bike and then go from there. I spend a lot of time just looking at the bike.

With Donnie's 300-tire bagger we changed the tank after I had it nearly done. I didn't like the shape and finally I asked Donnie what he thought. Together we decided it was too fat so I cut slots in the top, like a star and then pushed the top down so it didn't have as much arch. It's much slimmer now than it was before.

One of the things I like to do is embellish a basic shape. Sometimes I ask myself, 'what if I put a dash in the center or added an edge,' those are things I determine during the planning process. For a guy working at home there's an opportunity to make the part out of poster board first. Or to buy some foam and rough out the shape in foam so you know ahead of time that the shape works both in a practical and an aesthetic sense.

With a fender you can buy a blank, mount it temporarily on the bike and then run tape lines across the sheet metal or maybe use magic markers, to try the shape before you cut up that blank. It's another way that you can try lots of things on the bike without spending too much money or creating a lot of scrap.

The other thing is, when you tape it out or try a new fender or tank, be sure to put the bike on the ground, walk around and look at it from all the angles, so that whatever angle you look at it will fly, that it works. In a small shop you might have to roll the bike outside so you can get back far enough to assess the shapes you're working on. Careful planning can really save a lot of time later.

INSPIRATION AND IDEAS

If there's no customer, find a shape that you really like. I pick up a lot of ideas from guys around me, guys in the industry, other craftsmen. The actual shape I like might choose can come from a car or plane or whatever. I take notice of all kinds of things that aren't really motorcycle related. Donnie gets ideas for color from the fashion industry.

Within the motorcycle industry I get inspired by people like Jim Nasi, I am impressed with his bikes. And of

Once Rob placed the tank on the bike, it just didn't look right. So he cut a "star" in the top, pushed it down to take out some of the crown, welded it up and added a dash.

Early progress shot. The only true Bagger parts used here is the frame cradle under the TC engine.

9

The rear fender is from Russ Wernimont (RWD). "Russ makes a really nice product, the steel is a good grade and it's not under a great deal of tension, which is nice if you have to make any modifications."

course Arlen Ness and David Perewitz, those are people who inspires me.

In terms of the mistakes that people make, I think they start with a good plan and get off track. This happens more often with novices than with pros. The first-time guy needs to stick with a good solid plan. It might be good if they didn't read the magazines for awhile. What happens is half way through the project they change the look of the bike or the theme. That doesn't work, you need to have a cohesive plan and stay with it.

Especially when you're just starting out, you have to keep things in perspective. You should match your ability with your goals. You can't just jump in and do a gas tank from scratch. A lot of these guys have a strong interest, but before buying thousands of dollars worth of tools, take some classes at a Vo-Tech school. You can learn a lot and decide if you really want to do this before you spend all that money on tools and equipment.

The best tool is patience. Allow yourself to make mistakes and keep the expectations realistic.

This progress shot shows the partially finished bike. Rob constructed the head pipes early because they determine where the bottom of the bags will end up.

FINISH WORK

As you get better, you can do more finish work in less time. But you have to be realistic, you can maybe spend the time better working overtime at your regular job to help pay for the next project.

A novice looks at what I've done in terms of the finish work, and it looks simple and they get frustrated. Then they give up or they spend too much time on the finishing. It's more efficient to let the body guy or painter help with the finishing.

Have a plan, stick with it. Finish what you start. For whatever reason a lot of beginners give up near the end of the project. Like I said before, put together a good plan and then follow that plan to the end.

These days everything is disposable, I tell my kids someone is making this stuff, it doesn't have to be disposable, build something that is built by hand and that will be around for years and years. You can build something and take pride in it. A guy can make something that has value. Once you have the skills you are limited only by your imagination.

Copy & captions Rob Roehl

A good example of what Rob calls an embellishment - round rod silicon-bronze welded to the edge of the front fender.

When last seen, Rob had the tank finished, both fenders essentially finished, and the supports in place for the bags. The rear fender will be attached to the bag braces in at least 5 points on either side so the fender becomes an integral part of the frame.

Chapter Two

Rob's Tool Box

You Don't Need as Much as You Think

I've done some impromptu seminars and people are always surprised that I don't have more tools, it's really pretty basic stuff. You don't need this huge array of equipment. I think of all the guys who start out spending two thousand dollars on tools when they really don't need that much. If you're going to spend that much, go out and buy a good welder.

As you go along you accumulate tools and there's always the temptation to buy expensive

This is my junk drawer, filled with tools and anvils that I've accumulated over the years. I have a trailer hitch ball too. They're heavy, round, hard and cheap.

specialty tools. I've bought specialty tools, and found out later I could do the job without them. They do expedite the work so in some situations it may be a good investment, especially in a commercial shop.

I like the specialty mallets and I have a lot of T-dollies. With some creativity you can com up with a lot of specialty dollies. Even if you only use a particular home-made tool once, it's OK because you didn't go out and spend a boat-load of money.

I do believe in buying quality hammers, you get what you pay for. Spend money on a good DA, buy quality and it will pay off in the end. Like the material you use, you get what you pay for. Files are a good example, cheap files wear out fast, the good ones stay sharp a long time.

We don't show them here, but you also need some scribes, rulers and markers.

Yes, we do have a few power tools in the shop, like the band saw and a belt sander, but those are more about saving time, they aren't really essential.

These are just some basic dollies, in common shapes and sizes. On the top left is a spud dolly, which is popular because it has a variety of profiles. I like the little square one for corners, but most of my dollies are round ones.

I use these T-dollies, or post-dollies, daily. These are the most useful tools in my toolbox. I make them out of junk, usually for a particular job. I go find the right shape and weld that shape to a post and then use it to bend the metal around, a guy could have a hundred of these.

Copy & Captions by Rob Roehl

The wood mallets are the tools I use to put heavy shape in something. The leather slapper is good for rolling over edges.

The comma dolly on the right is one I bought and then welded to a post. It frees up one hand so I can move the piece over the dolly instead of having to hold on to the dolly. I do this a lot because it's one less thing to hold on to.

The plastic shaping hammers are from Covell. They're handy for knocking shape into something. I like the little pick end, which is useful for raising material by coming at it from behind.

These are my three main hammers that I use on daily basis. Of the two on the outside, one is dead flat, and the other has a slight crown. In the center is a flanging hammer which is good for rolling things over.

The shrinker and stretcher are pretty inexpensive tools that will save you a lot of time, especially the shrinker. I could live without the stretching but not the shrinker, it's a big bonus for a small shop. If I were setting up a shop, the shrinker would be one of my first purchases.

A look at the mechanism explains how the shrinker and stretcher work. If you're on a budget, you can buy just one "machine" and two sets of jaws, one to shrink and one to stretch.

This English wheel was built for me, note the wheel on top where it's out of my way...

...the wheels, which have varying degrees of crown, are also narrower than they would be for a more typical English wheel.

The English wheel is an advanced piece of equipment, even though it's prehistoric. This is a tool for the advanced metal shaper, and is especially useful where you're doing panel work. I tell people, 'Get one and spend the next ten years figuring it out.'

Chapter Three

Welding

Gas & TIG for Sheet Metal

To get a handle on the requirements for sheet metal welding, along with a short Welding 101 class, and a discussion of the pros and cons of steel and aluminum, we stopped in at Creative Metalworks in Blaine, Minnesota. While owner Kurt Senescall answered my questions, employee Pat Kary did a variety of welding demonstrations.

The demonstrations include TIG (or heli-arc) and gas welding applied to both sheet steel and

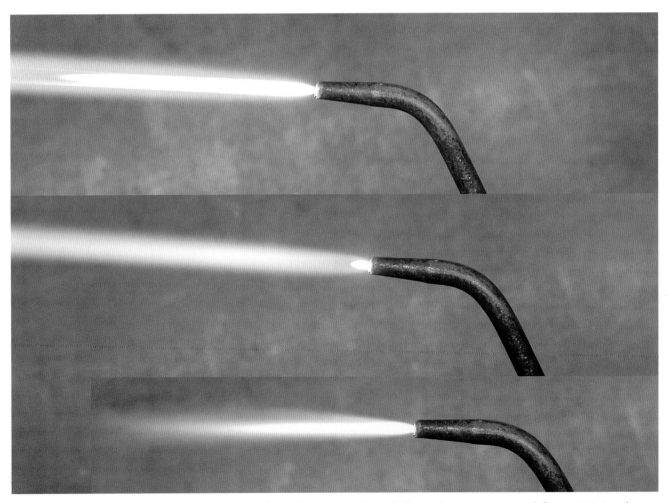

Top flame is a carburizing flame (more acetylene than oxygen), 2nd flame down is a neutral flame. Notice the large soft flame cone is gone. This is the flame used for most welding procedures. 3rd flame down is an oxidizing flame. You will hear a hissing sound if too much oxygen is introduced. This is the easiest way to notice this flame.

aluminum. Pat also did a short demonstration of silicon-bronze "welding" of steel. We left gas-welding of aluminum out of this series as Ron Covell did such a great job of illustrating those techniques in Chapter Eleven.

Today, most shops do their sheet metal welding of either steel or aluminum with the TIG welder. Yet, even an inexpensive or used TIG is about a thousand dollars. So part of the idea here is to illustrate the fact that while the heli-arc might be nice, you can indeed weld sheet metal with the old-fashioned oxy-acetylene welder.

Q&A, KURT SENESCALL

Kurt, What are the pros and cons of using steel for sheet metal fabrication?

Steel lasts longer, it's cheaper, and for a lot of people it's easier to weld. But on the other hand, it's harder to form. Some steels, like the aluminum or silicon-killed steel sheets, are easier to form, but cost more. These are drawing quality steels, created by adding a little aluminum or silicon at the end of the steel-making process. The net result is a steel sheet that's easier to form, but I don't think you really need these unless you're making really extreme shapes or using a die set.

What are the main pros and cons of using aluminum for sheet metal fabrication?

Kurt Senescall decided to open his own shop 16 years ago and he's still in that same building in Blaine, Minnesota, today. The dragster is a recreation of the Tom Hoover top fueler from the late 60's. The original was built by Woody Gilmore and bodied by Tom Hanna. The body is formed from .060 3003 H14 aluminum and welded with 1100 rod. Learn more at http://cacklefest.com/Hoover.shtml.

Here Pat has tack welded one end of our demonstration piece.

1. Then he tack welds the other end. It will take a few seconds for the metal to melt and a puddle to form. The size of the torch tip and the angle will put more or less heat on the panel.

2. Form the puddle, add rod, move.

3. One more time, form the puddle, add rod, move...

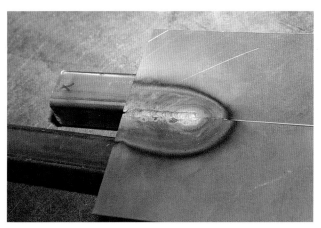

4. Hammer and dolly work on a gas weld is easiest when the metal is still hot. Again, only hammer and dolly as much as needed to relax the metal.

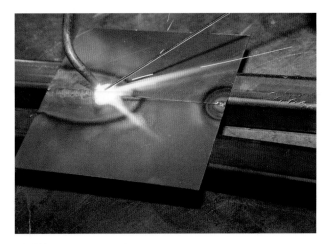

5. The process continues.

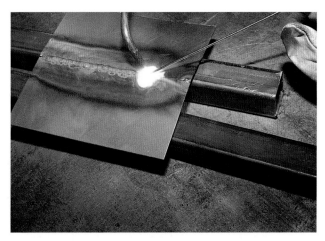

6. Notice the tacked end. Tack the panel every 4 inches or so and then tack equal spaces between those tacks before starting the solid weld.

3. Notice Pat is working the weld. Since the weld caused the distortion it is the place to work to relieve it.

Aluminum is easy to form and can be polished, but it's harder for some people to weld. Typically you are using thicker material than you would with steel so you have more material to work with when you get to the sanding and filing stage. Aluminum is measured in decimals, the .060 inch material is a common thickness for fabrication projects. You can go thicker though and still have good workability.

In the end it's the end product and how it will be used that determines whether you use steel or aluminum. Aluminum bike tanks are easy to form but they tend to crack, so again it's the application that's important.

If I don't generally need the A-K steel for fabrication, what grade of steel do I want?

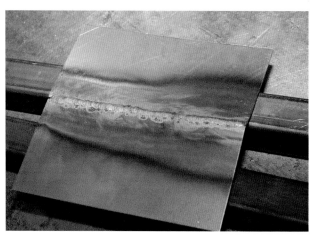

1. The finished weld, still hot from the torch.

2. This is a pretty small piece, but note how the shrinkage caused the seam to rise up.

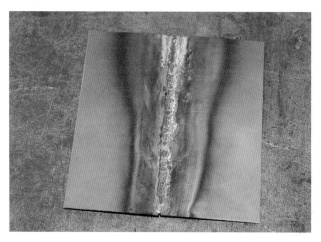

4. With a little work on the bead with hammer and dolly the bead is stretched slightly and the weld is relieved, the result is a flat piece of steel.

23

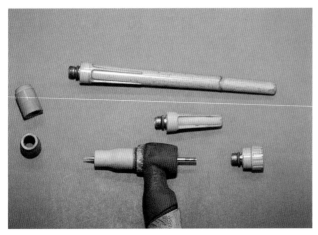

The torch can be made to fit smaller areas with a shorter ceramic cup or a shorter end cap.

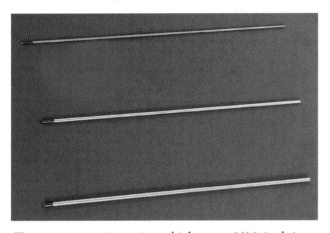

Tungstens come in various thicknesses. 3/32 inch is the most versatile. The 1/16 inch is used for very thin materials.

The point should be sharp. I use a longer taper than this for sheet material. The longer and sharper the point the more precise the welding can be.

Again, tack every 4 inches or so and then go back and tack between those tacks.

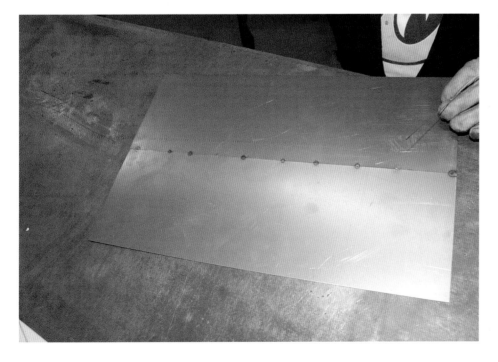

You want cold-rolled mild steel, the 1018 alloy in 18 gauge is ideal for most projects, 19 gauge is nice if you can find it. You do not want hot rolled, it's dirty and has a scale on the outside, which you have to clean off before you can start fabricating. I always buy my steel from a good supplier and tell them I want steel made in the US of A. Some of the sheet metal from overseas is brittle and will crack when you bend it.

Kurt: What are some of the types of aluminum sheet commonly available?

The most common are, 1100 H14, 3003 H14, and 5052. The 1100 is pure aluminum, so you can form it easily. In terms of strength the 1100 is the weakest. Also, it does not work harden, while the others do. Sheets of 3003 are the most common, this alloy would be good for any kind of body panels or something like a gas tank. If necessary, you can anneal the whole sheet or just one spot.

What about the hardness designation, the "H-14"?

The hardness designation differs depending on the alloy. For the 3003, H-14 is considered half-hard. Zero would be dead soft. I explain to people that the hardness is the property of the material, while tempering is something that was done to the material after manufacture. For this type of work it's good to avoid tempered material.

What are the advantages of using the TIG or heli-arc for welding in place of a gas welding outfit?

With TIG everything is cleaner and stronger. The heat-affected-zone is smaller, as a result you tend to get less shrinkage of the sheets. For welding aluminum there is a big difference between TIG and gas, the TIG is a much nicer weld.

Let's talk about the tungsten you use for the TIG, and do you always use a sharp point on the tungsten?

You can buy pure tungsten, I like 2% thoriated, it's radioactive and you can tell these from the others by the red ring around the end. This

With the tungsten about 1/16 to an 1/8 inch away from the panel, start the arc, add pedal (heat) until you form a puddle   then add rod, move, form puddle, repeat.

Work the weld area as you go.

Weld in about one inch or shorter increments. Hammer and dolly. Repeat..

Shopping for a TIG at MWS

For more information on welders and TIG units in particular we spent an afternoon at the Mississippi Welders Supply Co. store. The company has 8 stores, we spent our time with Troy Elmer in the Hudson, Wisconsin location. During the Q&A with Troy he pointed out the best values in welding equipment and some of the features to be found on the newest TIGs.

Troy, are TIG welders getting more and more common, especially among home users?

Yes, especially in the last 5 years. There are more reasonably priced models on the market now than there ever have been.

Can you describe the machines that a person at home or in a small shop might consider buying?

A basic DC (direct current) TIG welder starts at $900.00. This is what I call a thin-gauge machine, it doesn't have enough power to weld heavy material. You are limited to 12 or 14 gauge steel or stainless, no aluminum.

For about two thousand dollars you get a full feature machine. This machine will have DC and AC, that way you have the AC for aluminum. For the extra money you get the AC, you get higher amperage to weld heavier material. Another thing is the pulsing, this unit will have pulsing built in. And more money gets you a higher duty cycle.

We also have one machine at fourteen to fifteen hundred dollars that does have AC and DC, but no pulsing.

What's the advantage of pulsing?

Pulsing reduces the heat input, which is good for thinner materials, and it gives you a better-looking bead.

When you send a person out the door with the new welder, what do you recommend for a tungsten and rod, assuming they are going to weld sheet metal?

I recommend the 2% thoriated tungsten. In terms of rods, the 70s works really well for regular steel.

Do you offer classes for the people who buy a welder?

No, but all the local tech colleges do. They have really good night classes that cover all phases of welding.

Where do people make mistakes with a new TIG machine. And are there issues involved with the new welder that people didn't think about ahead of time.

For mistakes, sometimes they get the polarity wrong. Or they use the wrong gas. A MIG welder uses a mixed gas, a TIG should use only straight argon.

At Mississippi Welders Supply they stock a variety of welders, from relatively inexpensive MIG and TIG units to full-blown commercial units meant for a busy commercial shop.

Shopping for a TIG at MWS

The other hidden issue is the amount of power you need to run it. Most of the machines, especially the older ones, use a transformer and they require a pretty heavy circuit. Our midrange fifteen hundred dollar machine needs a 50 amp 220 outlet and the two thousand dollar machine needs 55 amps.

There are some machines that use an inverter instead of a transformer and these don't need such a heavy circuit, and they're lighter machines as well. An inverter machine with the same capacity as our midrange machine only needs a 20 amp 220 volt circuit. Some of these will run on more than one voltage source, like 220 single or multi-phase, even 110 volt, but only if you have a 28 amp 110 circuit. The inverter machines do cost more, two hundred to a thousand dollars more than a similar transformer-equipped machine.

You don't have to buy a TIG. A small setup like that shown fits easily on a shelf in a small shop and can be used to weld both steel and aluminum.

How do you feel about the various brands of welders?

We sell Miller so obviously we like Miller. I tell people to buy one of the big three, Miller, Lincoln, or Thermal Arc, because all are made in the US, you get better service and warranty, and if there are any problems it's easier to get parts or service later.

What about gas-welding outfits, how much less are they?

Quite a bit. The small setup we have on the counter with the small tanks is two hundred and ninety five dollars. And If you buy the Smith Tuff Cut, it's about five hundred dollars including the standard tanks and a cart.

The Econotig from Miller is a good welder for a small shop and offers both AC and DC operation and an output of 150 amps.

Hammer and dolly as needed after each weld. Doing this while the panel is still hot is easier but it can be worked cold…

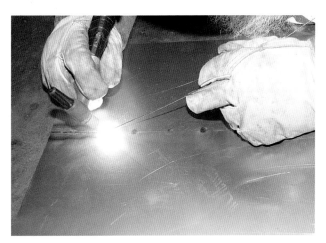

…another bead in process.

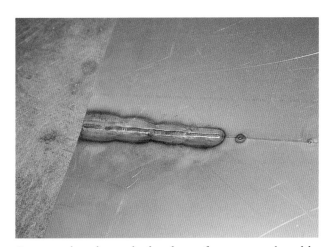

Progress shot shows the bead run from one tack weld to another.

Two demonstrations, one gas welded (upper) one TIG welded (lower). Notice the smaller heat-affected-zone in the TIG-welded example.

is a pretty universal tungsten. Rare earth tungstens are very good for aluminum if you can find them.

I always sharpen to a long tapered point, some say "ball" the end, but the point does burn back by itself if it needs to. It is easier to control the weld when you have a point, even on sheet aluminum.

What rods are available and commonly used to weld aluminum, and does the alloy of the rod need to match the alloy of the sheet?

Typical aluminum rods include 1100, 4043, and 5356, and these come in typical sizes. The 1100 is pure aluminum, so it's the most ductile. This is good if you need to hammer on the bead, or flatten the bead, but the seam is not as strong.

The 4043 is useful for lower grades of aluminum, like castings for example. This would be

Pat Kary spent many years doing production welding and much prefers the relative freedom of fabricating and welding street rod and motorcycle parts.

good if you are welding a Harley head.

The 5356 is a higher grade aluminum rod. This is good for sheet plate, and welding good grade aluminum and billet aluminum. The 5356 provides the best color match for anodizing if that's a consideration. Don't use base metal as rod, welding rod is meant to be rod, the alloys in the base metal are not meant for welding.

What about the rods used for heli-arc welding steel?

There are two basic steel rods, one is oxy-weld65, the other is ER70s, they are very similar, but come from different manufacturers. The number indicates the tensile strength. For example, an 80s D2 is a good rod for chrome moly, and has a higher tensile strength. For mild steel though I use the oxy-weld65 or ER70s.

You can also use silicon bronze rod. The advantage is the low temperature, you don't melt

...weld again...

...and hammer again.

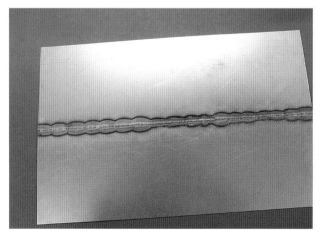

The end result is a nice, neat bead that's strong yet exhibits very little warpage.

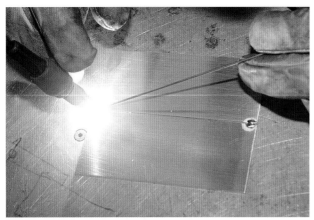

1. Aluminum may take a bit more to heat before a puddle forms because it dissipates heat so rapidly. Scotch brite or clean all areas to be welded including the welding rod before you start!

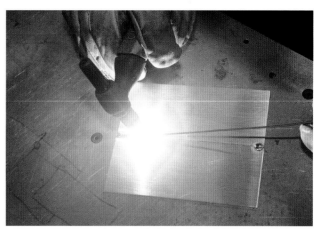

2. Again, like steel, tack about every 4 inches, then tack between the tacks before welding.

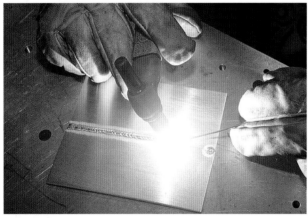

3. Unlike steel it is actually easier to hammer the weld flat after the welding process has been completed.

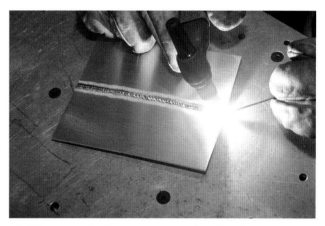

4. If you touch the tungsten to the aluminum or touch the rod to the tungsten you must resharpen the tungsten. Otherwise you will contaminate the weld, and have a harder time controlling the arc.

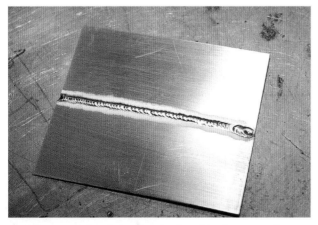

5. The top side of the finished weld, the next photo shows the back side - aluminum welds may not penetrate all the way through.

6. Penetration is important - If you plan to metal finish or hammer the weld flat you should weld the back side also or it will crack. Scotch brite or clean the back side before welding.

the base metal. You can't use this for butt welds, only when the metal overlaps or you are doing a T-weld. The silicon bronze almost sweats in like soldering. This would be good for any joint that needs to take vibration. A silicon bronze weld will hold body work well, and also holds chrome. It's available in all the standard sizes, starting with .030 inch, then 1/16 inch and all the rest.

With silicon bronze there is no flux, so there's no contamination for any process that comes later. This is good for header flanges or where a tube goes over another tube with a snug fit.

Is there a general rule of thumb for choosing the size of the rod?

As a loose rule of thumb, the rod should match the thickness of the material. Also, the width of the bead should be twice the material thickness.

Where do people make mistakes when they weld sheet metal?

They forget to use quality materials and they are not careful enough about cleanliness. You can't have any paint, rust or Bondo on the metal. And always buy good steel from a good yard, never use hot rolled steel.

Captions by Kurt Senescall

A finished silicon bronze weld. Note the weld looks like bronze and not burnt. Overheating will cause the weld to turn black or charcoal-looking. These silicon bronze welds are very durable and strong and take vibration and flexing well.

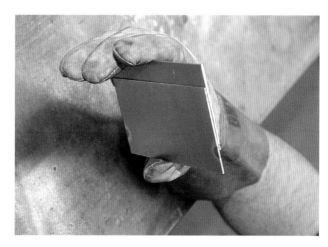

Silicon bronze is an excellent and easy rod to work with. Never use for a butt joint though.

Low heat is used. Use just enough heat to let the rod melt to the base metal.

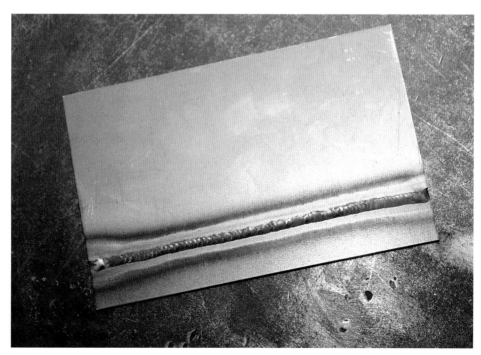

Chapter Four

Dog Dish

Basic Stretching and Shrinking

Making a "dog dish" is a typical assignment in any beginning sheet metal fabrication class. The project can easily be performed with a minimum of tools, and relies on stretching for most of the shape. As Rob says, "stretching is what's easiest to do at home."

The first thing Rob does is wipe off the coating of oil. Next come the first blows from the torpedo hammer. "I like the wooden hammers better than plastic," explains Rob. The one "power tool" that is used is the small shrinker. As Rob explains, "I find shrinking the edge frames the project, it

A simple disc formed into a dish is a very good example of several shaping techniques.

2. I begin with a round face mallet made of hickory. I prefer wood to plastic but success can be achieved with either. As you can see I am working the disc into a 12 inch leather bag filled with sand.

gives it definition so it isn't quite so much like a potato chip with all that tension."

The work with the torpedo hammer and sand bag result in a lot of stretching and walnuts. Rob uses a softer, smaller hammer to work out some of those walnuts. Next comes more shaping with the wooden hammer working over the dolly, and then Rob starts to work just inside the lip, "to try and make that part of the curve more even."

In terms of working with the hammer and dolly, Rob explains that there are really two techniques being used, "When I'm 'on dolly' hitting the high spots with the hammer and holding the dolly directly under it, this gathers up the area at the peak and it's really half shrink and half stretch. When I'm 'off dolly' the dolly is not directly under the area I'm hammering, then I'm definitely gathering up the metal."

Near the end Rob uses a slapper instead of a hammer to even out highs and lows. You can see the shiny spots are the highs, the gray areas are the lows. "The hard part is the finishing" says Rob. "I like to really finish the metal, but I'm a minority."

Captions by Rob Roehl

1. We start with a 16 gauge steel disc. I've marked it to roughly show where we will work the two techniques.

3. I prefer to begin in the middle and work to the outside.

4. With just a little effort, mostly in the center, you can see it's picking up shape.

1. Back on the bag for more shaping.

2. Continuing to work from the center to shape the disc.

3. Using my hands, I apply pressure to maintain a consistent shape.

4. After a little more hammering I've stretched a bumpy crown in the disc.

5. Moving to my post dolly I use a wood slapper with a leather face.

6. Here I begin to roll down the edges.

The edges can also be formed with a mallet and a hard surface.

Continuing the mallet work I choose a wider head. Inset: My favorite wood mallets.

Now I start to use my hand shrinker to pull down and gather (shrink) the edges.

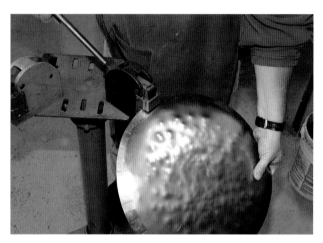

The hand shrinker quickly pulls a lot of shape into the edges.

After just a little work we have generated quite a bit of shape.

Then I continue the mallet work to achieve more shape.

Using the mallet against the table I begin to work out some of the lumps.

Some hand adjustments.

Again, I work the edges on the post dolly.

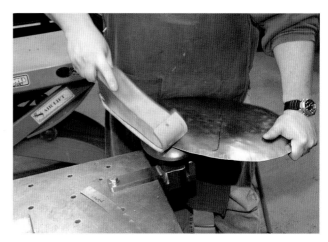

The slapper work on the dolly will continue to shape the edges.

For the sake of time I'll divide the disc and work in quarters.

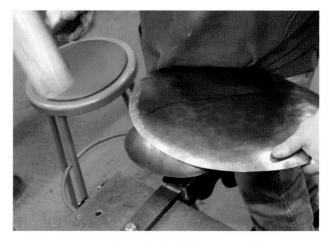

I continue to work with the dolly and mallet to begin smoothing out the lumps.

For finish work I will use a metal slap hammer. It has a slight crown.

Working on the post dolly I'm knocking down the lumps and raising the low spots.

The slapper is used to even out the edges and pull them down.

Continuing the work with the slapper smoothes out the lumps on the disc. The amount of finish is completely up to your amount of effort and patience.

It's easy to see how with a little "elbow grease" the slap hammer has smoothed out the one side considerably.

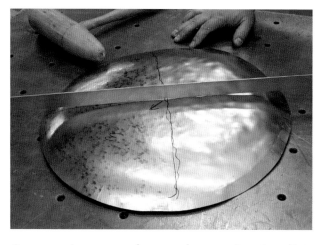

I can continue to work as much crown into it as I desire by pounding in more shape.

Chapter Five

Tank Tails

Extend and Enhance

Making a tank from scratch is a tall order. Even with the current renaissance of metal shaping there still aren't very many people who can make a nice looking, traditional gas tank from scratch. You can take a short cut and make a tank from stamped blanks, but it's still a lot or work and carries with it

the potential hassle of making sure the seams don't leak. The easiest way to change the shape of a gas tank is to add what are commonly called "tails." By extending the tank you can enhance the shape and stretch out the whole bike. You are afforded an opportunity to have the tank reach down and nearly

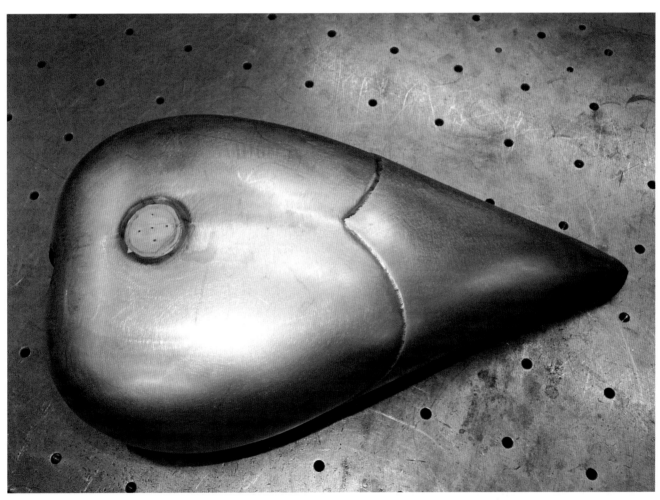

A custom stretched tank ready for body work and paint.

meet the side covers. And you can do all of this without any worries about whether it will hold gas.

PAPER PREDICTS METAL

Seen here is another Rob Roehl project done on a customer bike. The first step is to make patterns with poster board. This is both a chance to try out a number of different designs and to create templates that can be used to cut the steel. Rob uses magnets to hold the templates on the tank, and then stands back to ensure that he likes the shape.

A band saw is Rob's preferred method of cutting the steel, but there's no reason a saber saw or tin snips couldn't be used for this task. As Rob gets ready to cut the steel he comments that, "I tend to leave everything a little large so I have plenty of metal to work with." The metal is the typical 16 gauge cold rolled steel often used for projects like this. There's no real need for heavy material as these tails are not load bearing.

Rob starts by rolling the metal, the stretching and shrinking will come a little later. The majority of this work is done with the slapper working over a specialized and home-made T-dolly that's really nothing more than a piece of pipe with an extension that makes it easy to mount it in the vise.

In fact, Rob uses more than one home-made T-dolly. Number two is curved which makes it easier to create a tight roll along the bottom edge of the tails. The wooden slapper is used for much of this, the leather face means the slapper doesn't mark up the metal so there is less finishing work to do later.

The hand shrinker is brought into play to tuck in the edges where the tails meet the body of the tank. As the photos show and the captions explain, much of this is a matter or moving the metal in very small steps until the desired effect is achieved.

As Rob moves through the project he's not afraid to simply bend the sheet metal by hand over another dolly. Then it's a matter of more shrinking and more rolling with the wooden slapper.

When one side is finished Rob starts on the other. All the things he's learned about making this particular shape means that the left-side tail takes much less time than the right. And once the two sides are formed and trimmed to butt up against each other, it's time to start into the welding part of this project.

continued page 46

After positioning the tank, start roughing out a pattern in posterboard.

Next I cut out the rough pattern.

Rolling it on the edge of the table will shape the poster board.

1. *This gives you an idea of the initial shape.*

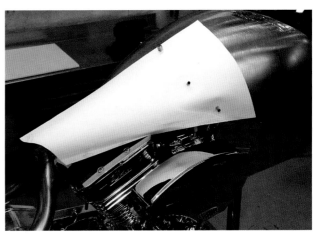

2. *The use of magnets will hold the pattern in place.*

3. *Refine the shape of the pattern until I'm happy, and then transfer the shape to steel.*

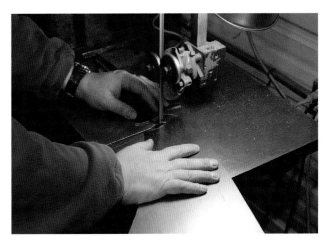

4. *Using a band saw I cut out the panels.*

5. *Deburring the panel with a belt sander cleans up the edges.*

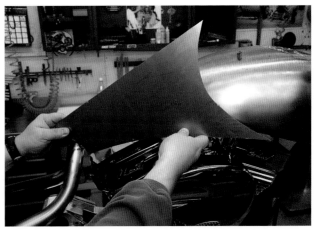

6. *Here's the panel "in the flat."*

The shaping begins with a T-dolly and a slapper.

Here you can see the main roll of the panel is being worked into shape.

I continue shaping the panel until it has a rough curl.

It's important to test fit the panel often to monitor the progress.

This area is marked and will require some shrinking.

The panel is patiently worked into shape with the slapper.

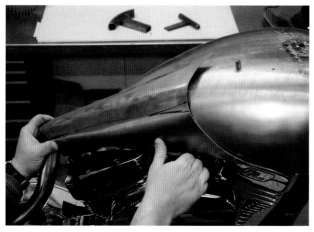

Another test fit and you can see the shape of the panel progressing.

One of my many T-dollies made of shop scrap. You can never have too many.

Using the slapper, the edges begin to form.

Here the inside curve is finessed.

The edge needs to be worked with the slapper.

I'm adding more curl, you can see the panel begin to really take the shape of the tank.

The center section can be tricky to shape.

Here's another test fit, you can begin to see how the panel is forming to the tank.

This view shows how the panel is beginning to take shape.

I do a little shrinking to add more curve.

At the front we are shrinking in order to pull it down.

Time to check the fit again.

2. The process is repeated on the other side to form a matching panel.

3. Carefully fit the two panels and trim the seam to fit.

4. Now the two panels can be tack welded together.

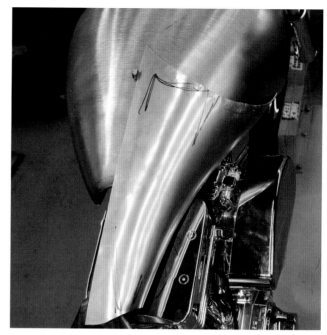

1. A low setting can be used when tack welding so you don't warp the steel too badly.

WELDING

Rob always says, "if you want a nice weld you need to have really nice fitment between the two pieces of metal." In this case the two halves meet perfectly along the top of the tank and Rob uses another small magnet to hold them in place during the first few tack welds. Gradually Rob adds more tack welds, some are fusion welds and some use a small amount of rod.

You will notice that the tack welds get closer and closer together until they are spaced only about one-half inch apart. Before the final welding starts Rob takes the tail assembly off and massages the seam on one of the post-dollies. The idea is to get the seam perfectly flat, to make sure the two pieces of metal are at the same level, that one didn't "jump" up and over the other as a result of the heating and shrinkage that occurs during the welding. If one edge does end up higher and overlapping the other, it must be dealt with before moving ahead with the welding and finishing process.

Once the two halves are joined as one, with a finished seam, Rob does a little additional finishing to the new assembly to ensure a good fit. Only after he has the seam finished on both sides, and the new piece fitting snug up against the tank does he tack weld the tail assembly to the tank.

The setting on the welder only controls the maximum output, the actual amperage is controlled by the foot control.

Now I can tack weld the center seam.

It's a good idea to check the alignment before getting too far along.

More tack welding down the center of our extension.

I skip around with the tack welds, always watching the alignment of the seam.

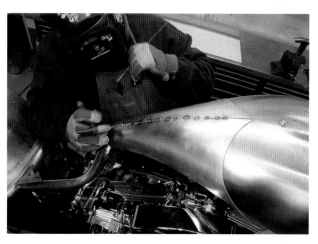

I like to have a tack weld every 1/2 to 3/4 inch.

  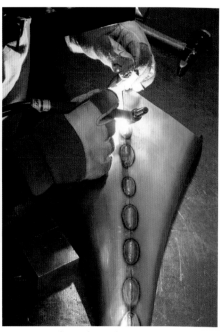

Raising the low spots is done from underneath. Again, it's nice to have the piece off the tank.

Now I can begin stitch welding the seam.

Care needs to be taken, I weld only about an inch at a time.

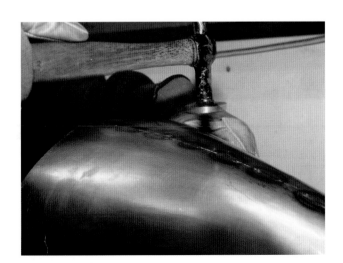 

Work the weld seam as you go.

Check the fit and seam shape again to assure a good fit.

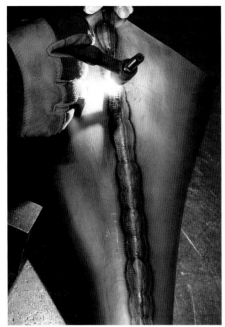

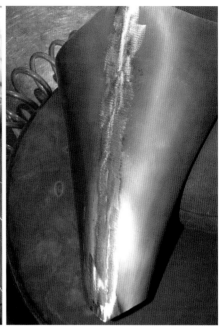

2. Finish welding the seam.

4. Remove any extra weld with a disc grinder.

5. Here's the seam after I've knocked down the weld.

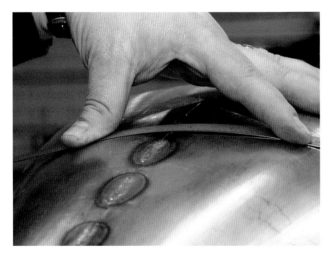

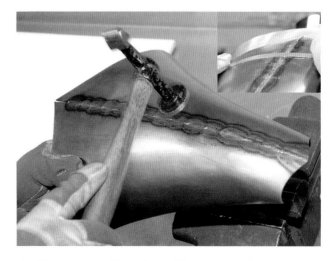

1. I like to check for lows before going any further with the welding.

3. Here I'm working the weld seam.

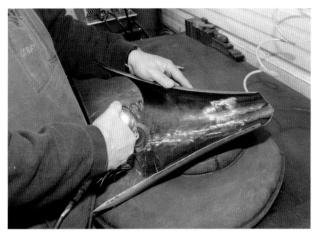

It's important to clean up the back side of the weld.

A slapper will smooth the panels and the seam.

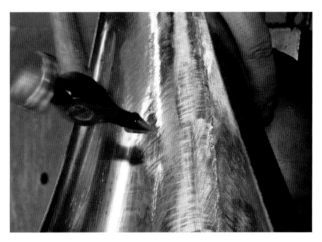

Raising a low spot can be done with a pick.

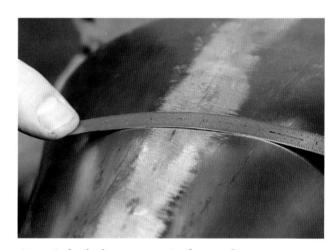

Now I check the seam again for any low spots.

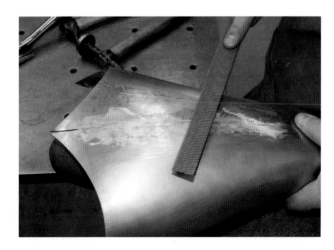

The welded seam is filed to help find any high or low spots which can then be smoothed out.

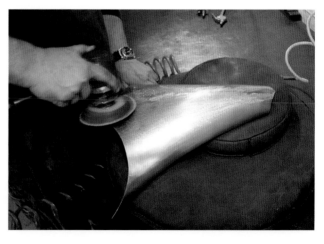

I finish sand with a D-A sander and a 80 grit disc.

The shape is checked again and is coming along well.

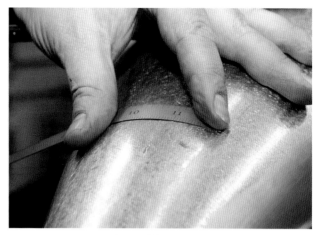

Here you can see the weld seam has just about disappeared.

I'm checking overall for fit and shape. Some adjustments still need to be made.

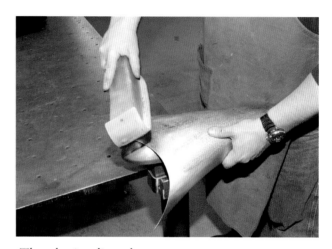

The edge is adjusted.

A little shrinking to the edge will fine tune the fit.

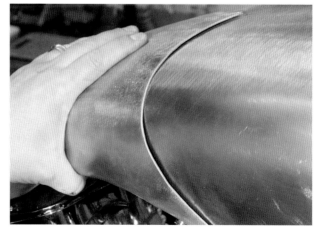

The edge is looking good now. Just a little more fitting will need to be done.

Now the fit is right on.

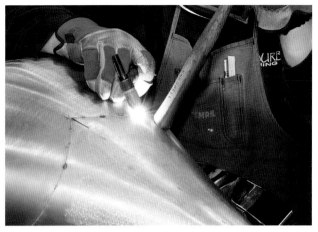

The tail is tack welded to the tank. Pressure on the hammer handle helps to keep the extension pushed up tight against the tank.

Working back and forth, from one side to the other, it's best to check your fit often.

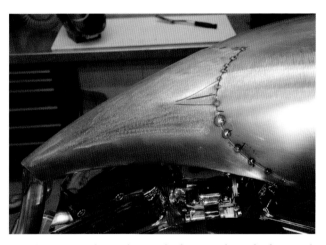

At this point the tail is tacked on and ready for stitch welding.

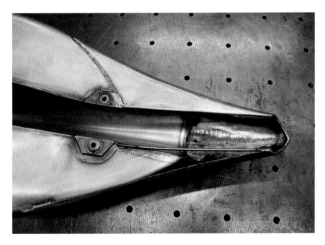

A nice finish to the tail, I weld 3/16 rod around any finished edges.

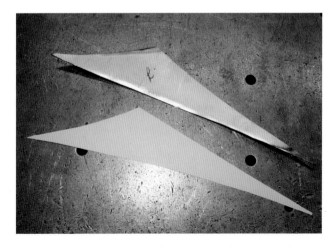

You'll want to cut some filler panels for the underside.

Here you can see how nice the second bottom filler panel fits before I start tack welding.

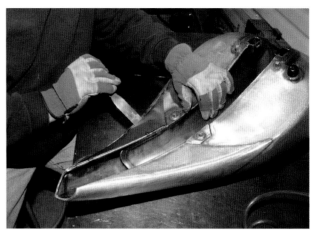

If the seam slips "out of alignment" during the tack welding, a putty knife can be used to get the seam aligned again.

Now I can continue to tack weld the panels into place.

Once tacked and correctly aligned I can finish welding the panels in place.

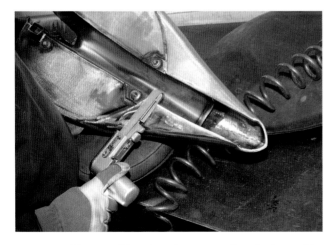

A Dyna file is really a handy way to finish the welds and clean up edges.

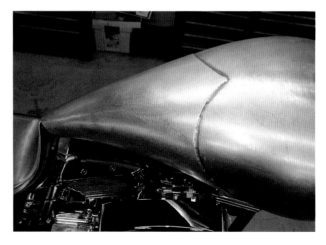

Bolted back into place, the tank can be checked once more for fit.

Chapter Six

Seat Pan

A Seat Base from Mild Steel

A motorcycle seat, be it a bobber, pro-street custom, or Bagger, needs a base that the upholstery or leather can attach to. Over the years seat bases have been manufactured from fiberglass, plastic and steel. Most custom builders use steel and the Donnie Smith Custom Cycles shop is no exception. Shown here is a relatively simple project of creating a seat pan from scratch.

Rob starts with a piece of light poster board. Actually, he starts with a folded piece of poster board. Once he has a shape that seems correct, the board becomes a template for cutting the sheet

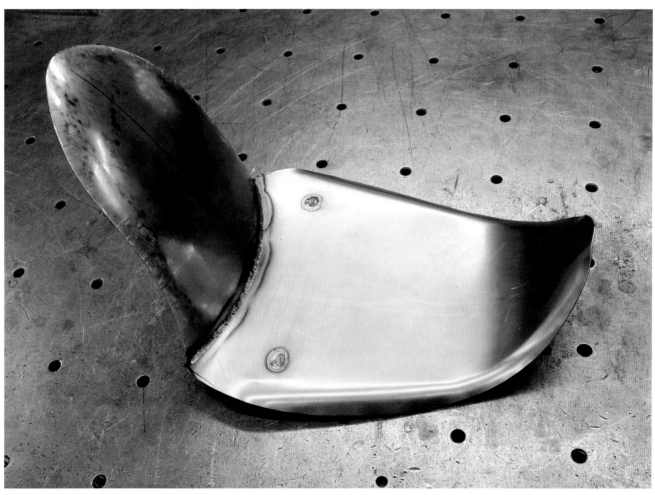

An example of a seat pan prior to being sent out to the upholstery shop to have it foamed and covered.

metal. Though some builders and seat manufacturers use suction cups or Velcro to hold the seat in place, Rob decides to bolt the seat pan securely to the frame.

A seat base like this would make a good first-time sheet metal project, as the shape is simple and requires mostly stretching and bending for its creation. The bending done here runs the gamut from the big radius bends done over Rob's knee to the more precise bends done by using the frame tube as a hammer form.

As is the case with many of the other projects seen in this book, the one "power tool" that makes it all go a lot faster is the small hand shrinker, used on the back of the seat to get the edges to roll in and hug the fender. Rob warns first-time builders to "be sure to leave enough room behind the seat for the upholstery, otherwise it will push the seat forward from the intended position."

Near the very end of the project Rob trims the two panels so they meet in a perfect joint, and then welds them into one piece using silicon bronze welding rod (see the welding chapter for more on silicon bronze). As Rob explains, "the silicone bronze rod is plenty strong and requires less heat. I don't have to put a bunch of heat into this and that's cool."

Captions by Rob Roehl

Then the pattern can be transferred to steel and cut.

I begin by making a paper pattern. The pattern is folded in half in order to get a symmetrical seat.

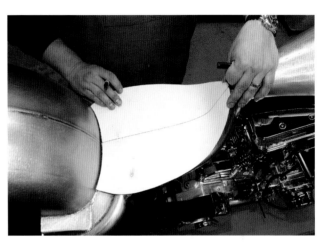

Check the fit and decide on the pan shape.

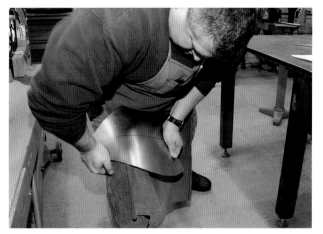

Using my favorite tools...

Now the pan can be checked for fit.

...I create a bend at the front and then add a little more curl.

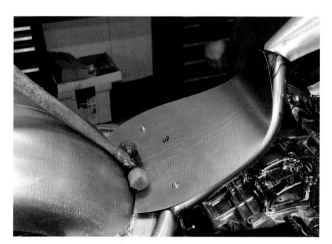

I check the fit again and bolt it in place to the frame.

I'm using the frame as a buck, the idea is to round over the edges using a rubber mallet.

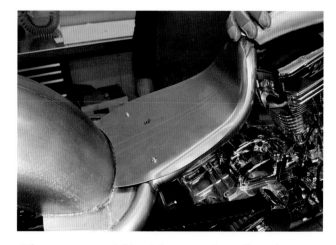

The seat pan quickly picks up a nice roll at the outside edges.

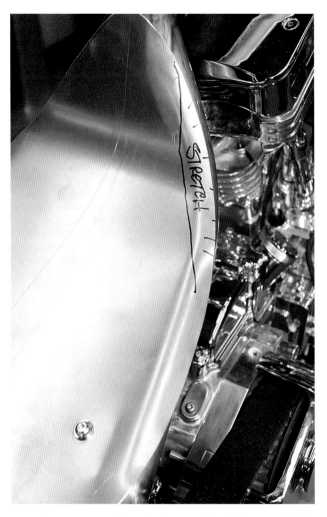

The bottom pan has shaped up nicely.

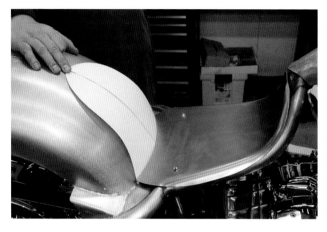

In this compound bend, the metal will be stretched around the frame tube.

Using poster board again for a pattern for the back.

Transferred and cut out of steel, it's a good idea to mark the center line for alignment purposes.

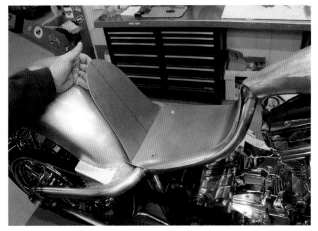

Getting an idea of how much shaping will need to be done.

I use my best tools and put the first roll into the steel.

Working the roll a little at a time.

Checking the fit, it's a good time to mark where to shrink down the edges.

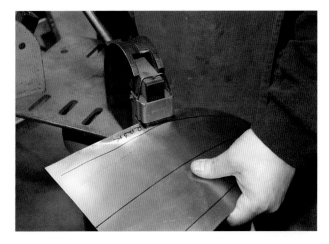

Use a hand shrinker to begin pulling down the edges.

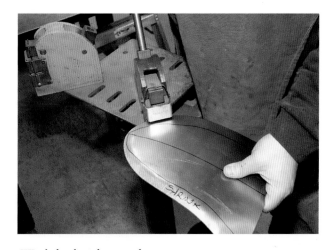

Work both sides evenly.

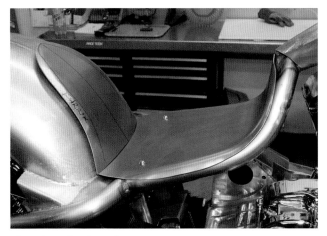

Another check to fit.

More shape is worked into the panel with a slapper and a post dolly.

A little more shrinking.

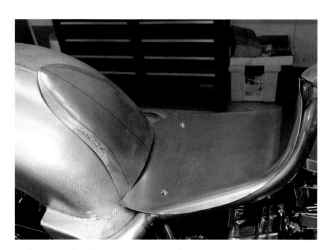

The panel is beginning to take shape.

Raising or stretching the center is best done on a leather bag filled with sand.

Smoothing the transition between shrinking and stretching, on a piece of wood with a wood mallet.

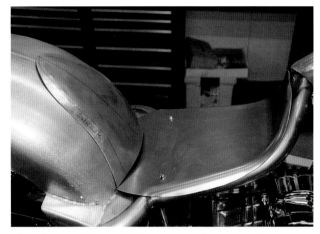

Another test fit and things are looking good.

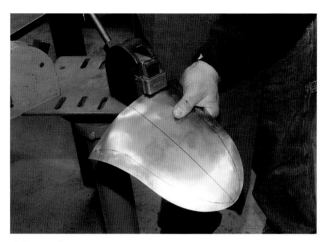

More adjusting.

A little more slapper work will smooth things out.

The panel fits well enough now to trim and fit.

Using a block, mark a cut line.

A tin snips is used to trim.

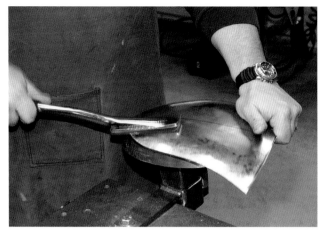

A little work with the steel slapper and the panel will have a smooth finish.

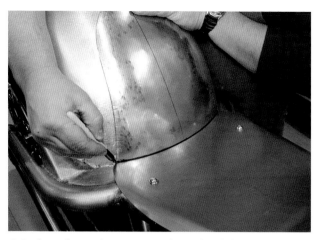

Mark and cut the seat pan for a final fit.

Everything should line up for a final fit.

Begin to tack weld the seat pins and the panels.

The seam and panels are welded.

Another double check for fit and the seat pan is ready to go out for upholstery.

Chapter Seven

Mount a Fender

Make it Sturdy and Provide Enough Clearance

Mounting a fender seems a simple enough task, too simple perhaps to qualify as one chapter in a how-to book. Yet, as with most "simple" tasks, there is a trick or two to doing this right.

First, tires get bigger at speed. Many a first time customizer came back from the first good road test shocked to discover that the paint had blistered off the fender (or worse) because at seventy or eighty miles per the tire grew enough to contact the inside of the fender. Friction makes

Mounting fenders on the bike may look simple, but an improperly mounted fender can ruin the entire look of a bike.

heat and heat will blister the paint. Lots of friction will do much worse. Rob positions his fenders a minimum of 1/2 inch off the tire by using a broken drive belt for a mock-up spacer as shown. He considers this the minimum amount of clearance, so don't think you can outsmart the guy who's been doing this for nearly twenty years.

Second, the position and shape of the fender are critical to the overall look of the bike. Spend time working on the position of the fender. As Rob says, "get the bike down on the ground and get back and look at it from a variety of angles." If there's any doubt about which fender to use, borrow an additional fender or two and try them on the bike. In this case, Rob started with a blank from Russ Wernimont and trimmed the fender blank to get exactly the shape he wanted.

Once it came time to do the actual mounting, Rob used one-off spacers between the fender and the fork, cut from billet by in-house machinist John Galvin. For the rest of us, similar spacers are available in various dimensions from the aftermarket.

During the mounting be sure to get the fender perfectly square. Rob suggests mounting one side, then checking the fender's position before drilling the holes for the second set of holes. Holes in sheet metal are more easily cut with a stepped drill rather than a common fluted drill.

When you do the for-real mounting after the fender is painted, be sure to use Loctite on the bolts so there is no chance they will unscrew. If there's any chance the mounting hardware could ever touch the tire use button-head Allens instead of a more common hex-headed fastener. Some of this is actually more important for the rear than for the front fender.

There you are, with a fender that sits far enough away from the tire to provide enough clearance. One that sits right and looks like it belongs on the bike. All you need now is paint.

Captions by Rob Roehl

The fender blank, fender spacers and an old drive belt used as a spacer.

I tape the old belt to the tire which ensures even spacing all the way around.

Next, I place the fender on the drive belt.

I position a spacer between fender and the fork.

I carefully marker placement with a permanent marker.

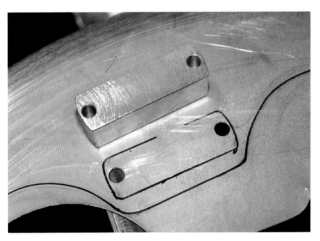

Then I drill the bolt holes and remount the fender.

After checking the alignment and fit, I finalize the profile.

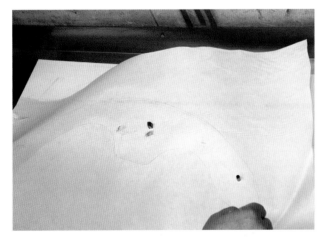

Here I'm making a cut pattern out of butcher paper using the "dirty thumb" technique.

Then I cut out the pattern.

Buying Sheet Metal

SHEET STEEL

When buying sheet steel you will first need to decide what to buy, how much, and where. Depending on your area the Yellow Pages is a good place to start. Try and find a supply shop willing to sell direct and also in small quantities. Find out if they will shear it into a manageable size. Ask them what is the minimum you can order.

I would recommend buying 1010 alloy or aluminum killed steel in .045 (186A) or .065 (166A). Some times it will be known as draw, deep draw steel or half hard. Buy the best quality you can find. Also, I use ER70S2 rod for the TIG welding sheet steel. If you can't find a supply house willing to sell you what you need, try calling your local hot rod shop or a local fab guy. Most guys

Sheet metal blanks created by spinning are generally under less stress than those created through stamping, but there is a seam running down the center - the best blanks are TIG welded.

I know will sell a chunk or two, or a least they will be willing to point you in the right direction. A couple of rules of mine are to always buy the best quality you can because in the end the time you save will be worth any added expense. Always clean your sheet before you work or weld it and don't be afraid to make some scrap. When in doubt use a heavier gauge.

BLANK FENDERS AND TANKS

I buy American made parts, I like the bigger heavier 12 gauge fender blanks, especially when I need the heavier structure like for a rigid-framed bike. I like these big fender blanks that are spun, the manufacturing process seems to put less stress in the metal. Spinning is nice too because they can change the shape and the dimension of the corner radius. The blanks from overseas seem to be under more stress, and the seams were welded with a wire-feed so it's hard to change the shape or modify those blanks. The two brands I like are D&D and Russ Wernimont (RWD).

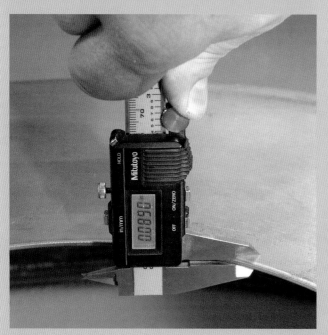

Heavy gauge blanks mean the fender will stand up to a lot of abuse.

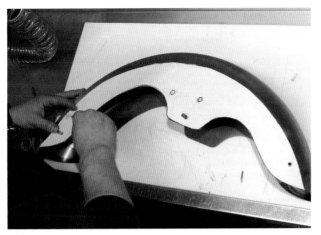

It's a good idea to test fit the pattern on the blank.

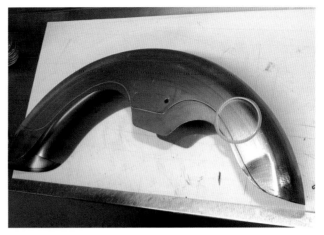

I mark the cut line with pinstripe tape.

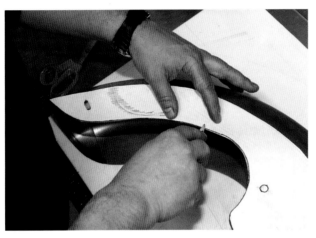

Then transfer the cut line to my pattern.

And here's the pattern with the marked cut line.

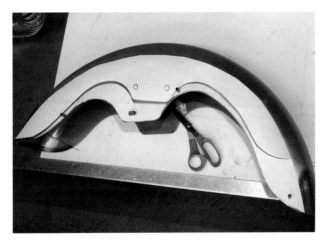

Next I cut out the cut line pattern.

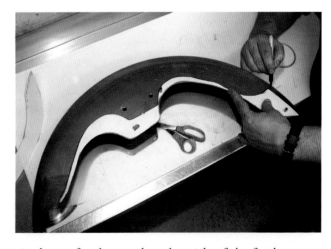

And transfer that to the other side of the fender blank.

With the tin snips I trim off the excess metal.

I am using an aircraft tin snips, it does a nice neat job with little distortion at the cut line.

I like to use the belt sander to clean up the edges.

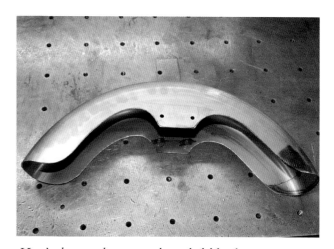

Here's the rough true and sanded blank.

I like to final sand the edges with a Dyna File hand belt sander.

Now I re-fit and check all the seams.

Chapter Eight

Air Cleaner Cover

Another Good First-Time Project

When it comes to building something for your motorcycle that is both aesthetically pleasing and relatively easy to create, an air cleaner cover is near the top of the list. The part is not load bearing, the shape is simple (depending on how crazy you get with the design) and it doesn't affect the operation of the motorcycle. If it falls off or you don't get it done for a month, the bike will still run.

Rob designed this teardrop-shaped air clean-

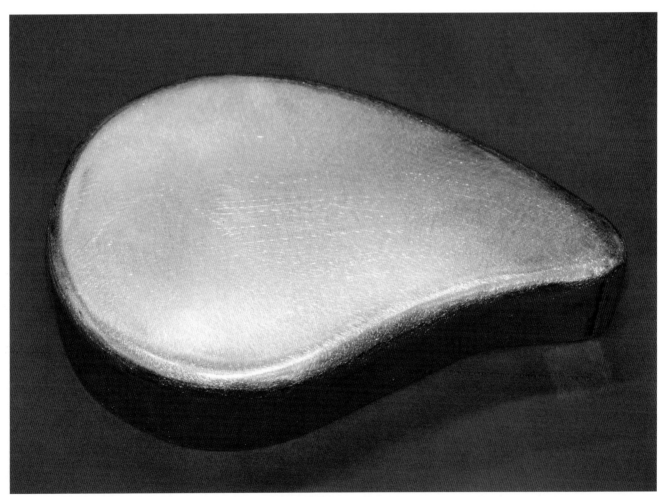

This simple air cleaner cover will add that custom touch to your bike and can easily be embellished to create an even more personal touch.

70

er cover because, as we just said, "it doesn't have a lot of shape, yet in the end it's a piece you can be very proud of."

THE STEEL

The material is the common 16 gauge cold-rolled steel. This is a demonstration project, so for the design Rob just starts out with a common K&N filter element and designs the cover to fit over that element. In the real world you will likely want the cover to fit over the outside of an existing round air cleaner assembly. The cover you make could be held in place on the round air cleaner with two-faced tape or Velcro or whatever fits your needs.

As the pictures show, Rob started by drawing a circle larger than the element and then added the tail. As Rob explains, "I drew out the tail in a shape that I found pleasing." The depth too is determined by the air filter element. Essentially this will be a two-piece part, which helps to keep it all simple.

ADD A LITTLE CROWN

"You could just cut out the flat cover," explains Rob, "and then roll the edge and weld it all together, but that's unacceptable. That would be a pretty crude looking piece." In this case Rob decides to add a little shape to the edge or corner of the air cleaner all the way around. The shape, or crown, he adds at the edge accomplishes two things: It gives the cover a much more pleasing shape, and the crown at the edges gives the sheet metal more strength and minimizes shrinkage and warpage during the welding part of the process.

Rob uses a couple of his favorite T-dollies and body hammers to create a crown all the way around first the long 2-1/2 inch side-strip, and then the flat part of the cover. "By being pretty patient as I hammer the edges over the dollies I avoid having the main piece (the face of the cover) want to curl. I want it to stay flat, if I did all this work in one or two whacks then it would want to curl."

continued on page 81

A simple sketch on poster board gets me started.

I've left about 1/2" around the air cleaner.

Here I'm measuring the element to find the width of the sides.

71

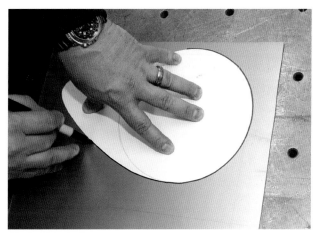

Next I transfer the pattern to steel and cut it out.

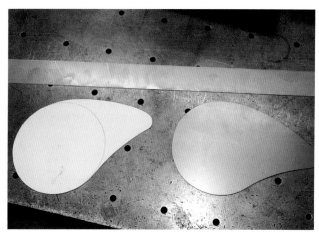

The face plate is cut out of 16 gauge steel.

Now I start a roll on the side of the strip.

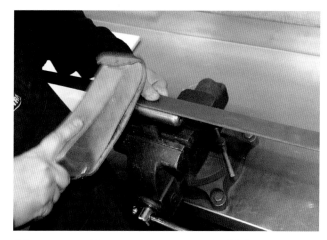

Here you see I'm continuing to rock all the way down the strip.

A closer shot of the half roll on the side strip.

Here I change to a big, flat, round post dolly made out of garage junk.

Slowly and patiently I work my way around the face plate...

...rolling the edge over the radiused edge of the dolly.

Beginning to roll the edge of the face panel.

You have to work the edge over gently.

I always try to keep the face as flat as possible.

Rolling over the edge on a reverse curve.

Using a T-Dolly to roll the small end.

The concave section at the bottom of the tail, the area with a reverse curve, is a hard area to shape.

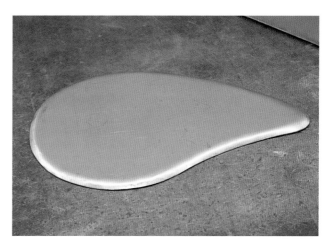

The finished cover with a nice crown all the way around. Note that it's still flat.

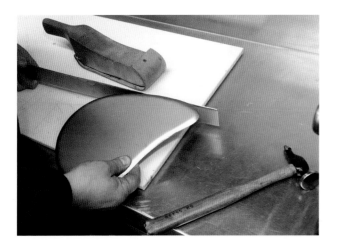

Deciding where to put the seam, I like to start on the tightest corner.

Here I'm rolling side strip on the T-Dolly using a wood slapper.

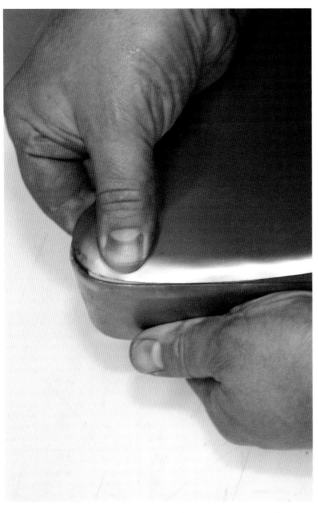

It starts with one tack weld.

It's important to match the side strip curve to the face plate.

Here you can see we have a good start to our cover.

Then I start to add tacks where the fit is good.

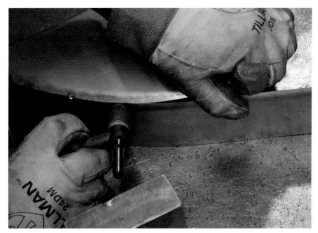

I continue the tack welds while working and holding the side panel in place.

More tack welds are added as the two pieces start to come together.

You can see how I wrap the side piece with my free hand while tacking.

Almost halfway done.

A little tune up on T-Dolly end to line up the two edges.

I continue to tack my way around. Patience, patience.

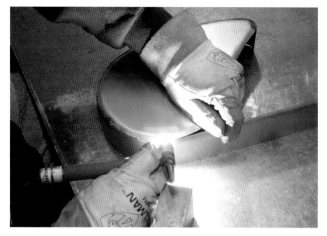

More tacking.

A little more hammer work. Now is the time to fix any bad fitment between the two pieces of metal.

Continue to work and align edges.

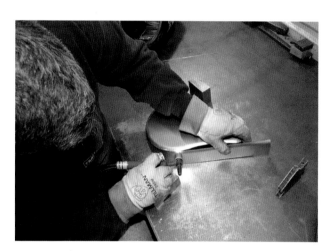

More tacking.

A little hand forming.

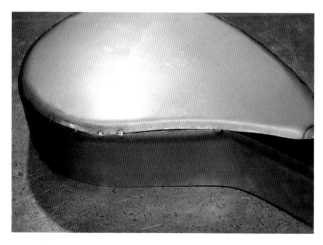

You have to just keep working the edges together.

1. More tacks in the concave area.

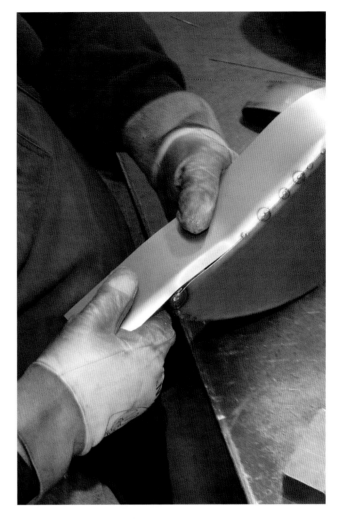

2. Checking the alignment.

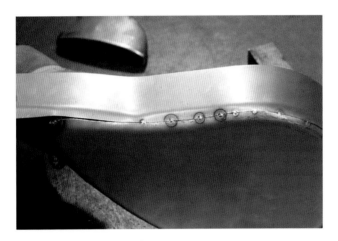

3. Working side panel on a reverse curve.

4. Marking the seam for the cut.

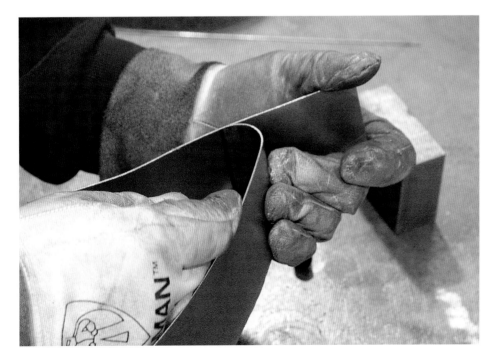

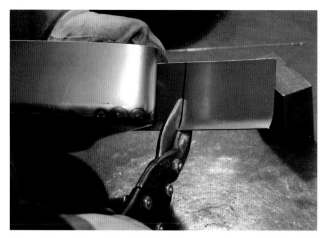

I cut the seam with tin snips...

...and then check the fit.

A little more work on the T-Dolly.

Here I'm tapping the seams down.

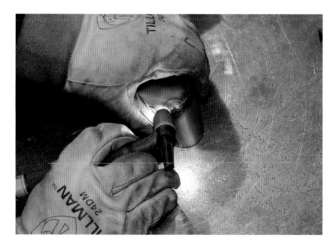

Now I can finish tacking the seam.

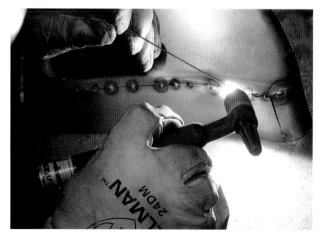

Here you can see how close together the tack welds are.

Finally the cover is tacked all the way around.

I check the alignment of the seams one last time.

If you have time to weld it - you have time to clean it first.

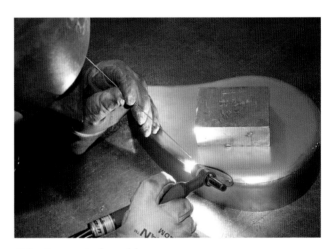

I begin to stitch weld.

Working my way around the cover, filling in as I go.

Here's the finished weld on the cover.

If you check the photos you see that the flat face did in fact stay flat even after Rob created an edge with a nice radius all the way around the perimeter of the piece. With patience he was able to do a lot of shaping without having the hammer and dolly work affect the metal except in the immediate area being worked.

WELDING

The TIG welder is set at 90 amps DC. Again, 90 is the maximum that can be applied, the real amount of amperage is determined by the position of the foot pedal. The first tack weld is a pretty good one because Rob is essentially going to roll this piece to make it match the radius of the cover. Making sure the side strip follows the shape of the cover is a matter of carefully positioning the strip, then keeping it there with a tack weld, then moving ahead and repeating the process. It's often necessary to stop and work the seam with a body hammer going back to the tack welding. "Working the seam like this to make sure it's smooth and that the edges are even saves a lot of time later. This seam will final-weld better, and once it's welded it will require less finish work."

Once Rob has the air cleaner cover tack welded together he backs up and starts cleaning the piece before proceeding with the finish welding. "The material must be clean," explains Rob. "You need to get rid of any rust or dirt. Even the oils from your hands will affect the final weld, so it's a good idea to get those off."

"The two pieces of sheet metal fit so nice you could almost fusion weld them together," explains Rob. "I don't worry about total penetration because this is not a load bearing part, I'd rather have a nice seam with minimal warpage."

Finishing the seam starts with a small air-powered grinder, which is used to take the top off the bead, and progresses to an 80 grit pad mounted to a DA. When Rob is done the part is ready for primer, a little more finishing work, and the final paint. A unique part that's relatively easy to fabricate and finish. One that's sure to add a nice touch to your motorcycle.

Captions by Rob Roehl

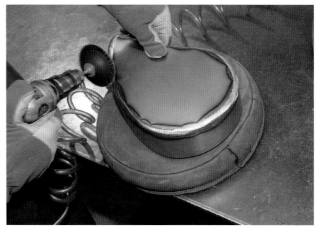

A quick hit on the weld with a small 36 grit disc.

I like to finish parts for paint with my 80 grit disc.

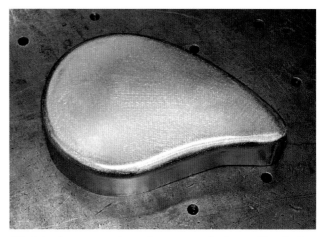

Finished cover ready to be mounted, then off to body work and paint.

Chapter Nine

Exhaust Pipes

Roll Your Own

The exhaust fabrication seen here is what Rob calls, "pretty straight forward. I'm using stepped pipes which is real common both for performance and a good look,

"I size tubing according to the size of the tubing. From 80 to 124 cubic inches I run up to 2-

1/4, or maybe 2-1/2 inch diameter. Unless the motor is really exotic the ports all start with 1-3/4 inch pipes.

In this case I start with a 1-3/4 inch length of 1-3/4 inch tubing. As you can see from the photos, I force the collar on the pipe then fusion weld

This is a good example of an exhaust for a right side drive 300mm tire bike. They are stepped and staggered to as close to equal length as possible for best performance.

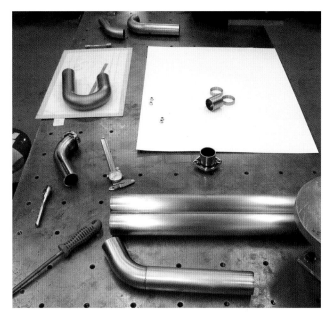

The workbench is prepared with some of the tools and parts needed to fabricate this exhaust.

Begin with a 3/4 inch diameter exhaust tube cut to 1 1/2 inch lengths. The exhaust flanges will be added to make the port sections.

The flanges tap on over the tubes, then I weld them on the inside to secure them.

Here we used common OEM flanges and slip rings, just like the stock ones.

it so it's a nice smooth port design with no restriction at the pipe.

"Because we use these machined collars, which we manufacture in-house, our pipes really snug up well to the port. The pipes are really solid the way they mount. For the flange and snap ring we just buy the standard aftermarket kits, though we do use a neat 12-point nut which makes it easy to get a small 3/8 inch socket in there.

"I tend to make the front pipe first. You can run a piece of tape ahead of time to see how you want the pipe to flow. I try to get something that will run parallel to the bottom of the frame and pick up the angle at the front of the frame. I like to figure out the finish point early, where the muffler or exhaust tip will be, and that way all I have to do is fill in the middle. In this case I decided to go from 1-3/4 to 2, and then finish with 2-1/4 inch pipe. Big magnets are really handy as a way to hold everything together during the mock-up phase.

"The way it works out, the 1-3/4 section will be 8 inches long, the 2 inch section will be 12 inches long and the final 2-1/4 inch section will be 24 inches long. This basic design has worked well in the past. It's a good sounding pipe that

continued page 86

2) An easy way to find a pleasing angle, use a tape line.

3) Here is an example of the direction for the bottom pipe.

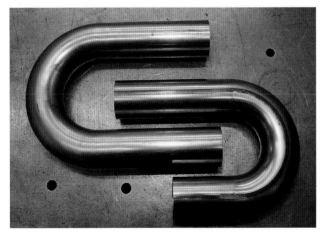

5) Shown here are U-bend and J-bend pipes. Pipes can be purchased in different diameters and bends to complete your exhaust.

1) The small port sections are bolted on the motor as a starting point.

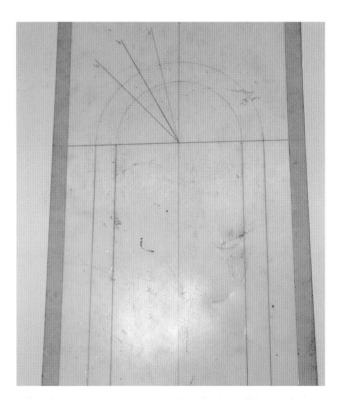

4) This is a simple cut graph which will keep the cut lines on center. Note that the center of the bend and the typical angles are marked.

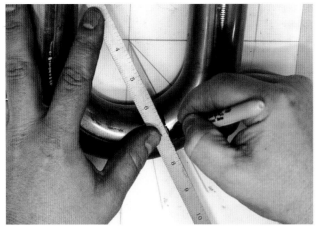

This is important to cut on center so it will match the next piece.

Here the pipe is marked for the cut.

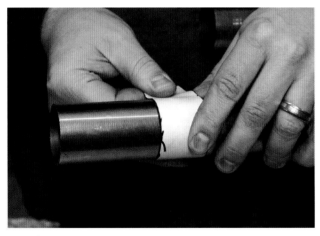

When you cut straight sections, a piece of paper wrapped around the tube will give you a straight cut.

I like to cut the tubing using a band saw.

I always flat-sand the tube after the cutting.

A finished cut, ready to match the next piece.

Here I'm fitting the first tube.

After the first tube is fit, it's time to figure out the next bend.

The distance between the two pieces is checked.

Shown here is a rough fit of the stepped pieces of tubing.

runs well across the rpm band. These particular pipes will not have any baffles.

"I start with U-bends from SPD Exhaust. You don't want automotive exhaust components, because they are aluminized. If you do buy automotive grade pipes you have to sand off the finish. This tubing from SPD is 16 gauge, 1100 mild steel. You can find 14 gauge but 16 is plenty heavy. If you buy the pipes all in the same gauge they slip-fit better. These are mandrel bent, otherwise they have a big flat spot in them, you can get them as tight as a 3 inch radius.

"Three to 6 inch radius bends are what I use most often. I made myself a cut chart out of poster board. Which is nothing more than a centerline squared off and then I drew the common bend centers on it and a couple of the common

continued page 88

Another check for length.

The first exhaust pipe is ready for a final fit.

To make a nice fit, roll down the edges.

Using an old piece of fork tube works well when I roll the edges of the tubing..

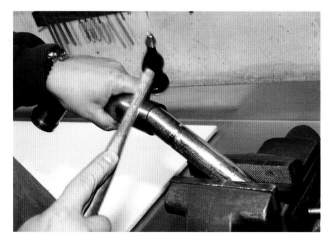

Simply hammer the tubes' edges until it fits tightly.

As you can see here, this makes for a really nice transition.

1. Magnets and tape can be used to hold the pipe in place.

2. Be sure to test all the surrounding parts so nothing is overlooked and there is plenty of clearance.

4. Time now to start tack welding the pipes.

3. One last check before welding.

angles. I cut it perpendicular to the centerline, if you don't you get a cut that isn't round, it's an oval. If you make really nice cuts you get a good match up between the two pieces of pipe and you get a nice weld with no gaps to fill. Don't sand the welds, let the polisher do that. The welds have to be nice because even with mandrel bends the metal is thin on the outside because it's stretched. I like to use the power saw and then sand it so it's dead flat, you could use a file too.

In terms of design, I use the exhaust pipes to frame the motor. A lot of high low pipes cover the motor and stuff that I like to see. Guys do these twirly exhaust systems and they put all these conflicting lines in the bike.

I want the bike to be one whole picture, not three or four separate pictures. The exhaust is a big part of the way the bike looks.

Captions by Rob Roehl

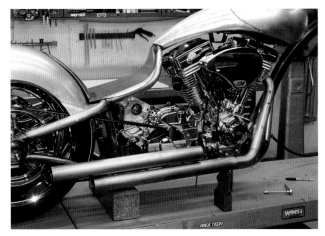

Here the next tube is roughly fit in.

A pipe from the rear head is positioned to fit...

...the second pipe will need to meet it.

The top pipe is fit again.

Back to the front pipe, I measure the length of the first step on the first pipe.

Mark the second or rear pipe to match the front.

Brackets

Slip joint mounts that were made in the shop.

A simple slotted plate will tie the pipes together.

Mounts bolted up and ready to mount.

A bungee cord helps hold the mount in place.

A mount tack welded to the back side of the pipes.

Made out of 1/4 inch bar stock, this is a frame mount.

Brackets

Here's the frame bracket tack welded to frame.

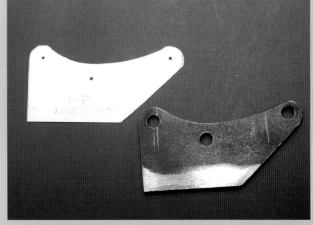

A simple cardboard pattern and steel cut out for the front bracket.

The bracket bolts to nose cone.

And attaches to the exhaust pipe.

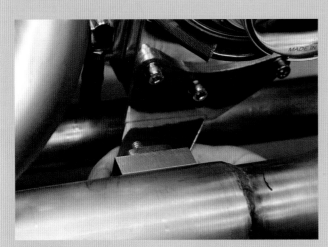

This is how it looks from the outside...

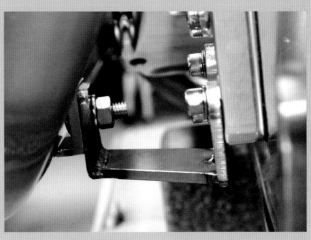

...and from the front.

Fitting, prepping and marking the first step on the back pipe.

Marking the pipe for the cut.

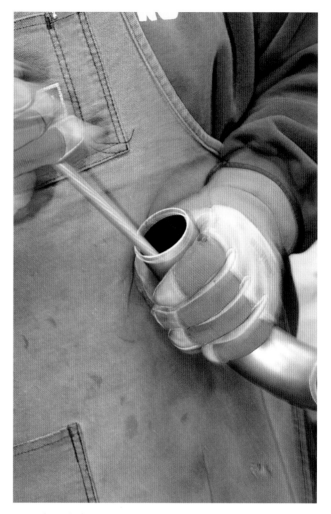

Sand and deburr all the cuts for a nice fit.

I cut the pipe using a band-saw. Whatever you use to cut the pipe, try and get a nice straight cut.

Here I'm preparing for the final fit.

I double check the fit of the rear pipe.

Again, roll the edges for a nice fit between the two pipes.

Notice how nice the transition is.

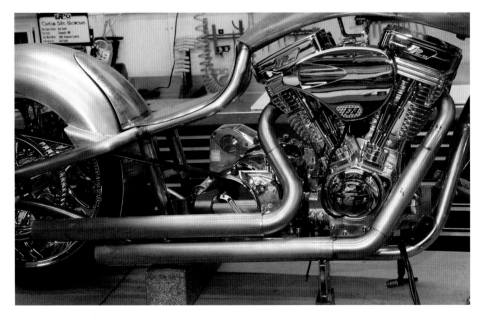

The pipes are fit and ready to be tacked, then the final welding completes the exhaust.

Chapter Ten

Fender Fabrication

First You Have to Make the Buck

When Bruce Terry agreed to make a demonstration fender for the book, he decided to go all the way. The fender isn't a little shorty bobber fender, but rather a full fender formed with the help of a buck.

Bruce starts this project by measuring the radius of a nearby motorcycle wheel, and comes up with a 12 inch measurement.

A piece of wire is shaped and used as a profile or guide, Bruce explains as he does, "you can

Perhaps a bit over the top for a basic fabrication book, the shaping of this fender includes the construction and use of a buck, a useful lesson for anyone contemplating more elaborate shaping projects.

draw a line with the guide and then flip the guide over and see if it's symmetrical. I decide the depth of the fender is 3-1/2 inches, so then we can draw in the bottom of the fender, the lip."

DRAW IT ON PAPER

Working from these known dimensions Bruce draws out a full size fender, and from that starts the construction of the buck. The side rails, made from 1X1/8 inch steel straps, are the first parts to be formed. Making the buck turns into a fabrication lesson all it's own, complete with a shrinking lesson for the side rails and the creation of a bending jig that makes it relatively easy to shape a series of identical curved ribs.

Building the buck is made easier by the full size drawing. During the construction Bruce works hard to ensure that the cross braces and the ribs are identical in dimension and shape. Much of the steel used for the buck is hot-rolled, which means the slag must be ground off the outside. "The slag is super hard carbon," explains Bruce. "It will contaminate the welds and it also gums up the jaws of the shrinker, which is why some guys buy nothing but cold-rolled steel."

"A lot of guys over-weld everything," says Bruce. "But all that welding causes too much

continued, page 99

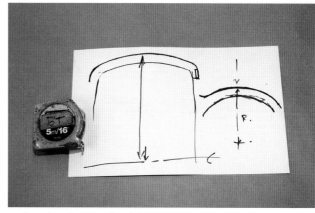

After deciding to build a custom Fat Boy rear fender, a rough conceptual drawing is done here. A cross section and side view are shown.

Now I'm ready to draw the layout full size with accurate radius and dimensions.

The radius of the fender is important so allow for enough clearance between the fender and the tire.

95

1. Here the exterior radius (O. D.) is drawn to illustrate the tire size.

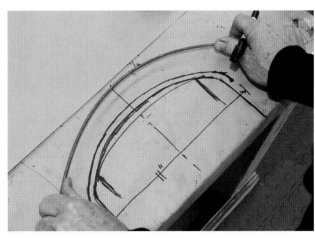

2. Using a steel rod, a smooth natural shape is created to establish the top radius of the fender.

3. Using a steel wire here I form a cross section as a 3D visual aid.

4. Then we look at a cross section and note clearance on the top and sides of the tire.

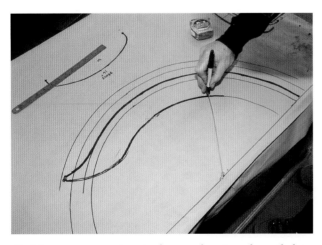

5. Now a cross section is drawn showing the stylish tail design.

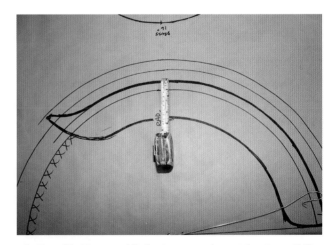

6. Finally I've established a complete side view, full sized drawing.

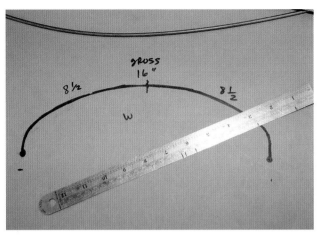

Then I measure out the full sized, cross section drawing in order to determine the materials needed.

A large pushrod tip is used to bring 1/8x 1 inch bar to red hot.

Here I am planishing/hammering the "cold" side of the bar to stretch the bar into the desired shape.

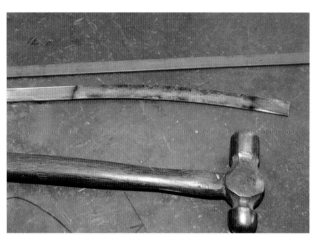

Using the "old school" technique to form this 1/8 x 1 inch bar stock, I heat shrink one side and hammer/planish the other to form a curve.

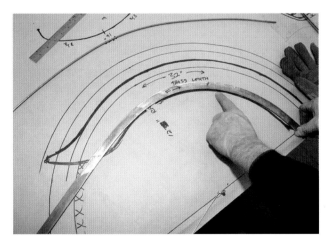

This bar is formed to fit the cross section drawing and will be used as one side of the station buck to be made.

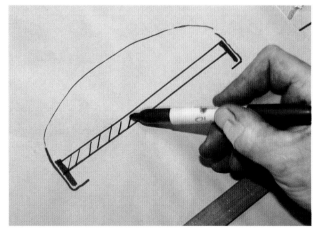

Now focusing on the buck design, a cross section drawing is being conceptualized.

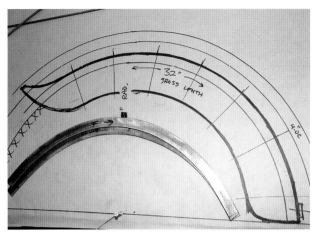

Now that I have one side of the 1/8 x 1inch bar, buck edge I fabricate a duplicate of the other side.

Here I am making sure the cross braces are all the same exact dimension.

Then the fabricated framework is checked against the cross section drawing.

After cutting the square tubes I start to tack weld them in place.

Now I check it all against the full-size drawing.

That leaves me ready to form the top curved ribs for the buck.

warpage, so I try to go with lighter welds as I weld in the cross braces and the ribs." One of the last parts of the puzzle to figure out is the tail of the fender. Once Bruce decides on a shape he comes up with a way to incorporate that shape into the buck. "I think the way I'm going to approach this is to form the center part of the fender first, then the two sides, so it will be made from a total of three pieces."

THE PAPER TEMPLATE

"Its amazing how much shape there is in this fender," explains Bruce. "Anything that has an arch to it and is a compound curve has a lot of shape. The paper template shows you how much shape the piece has, and can be used as a pattern when you cut the metal. The degree of overlap where I do the slits shows how much shrinking you will have to do. If there were areas where you had to cut slots and the slots in the template end up spread out, that would show the areas that need to be stretched."

The material is 3003 aluminum and Bruce anneals the aluminum in order to make it easier and faster to shape this fender. "You should almost be able to see through the layer of soot," says Bruce, "and then heat the metal enough that you burn off that soot. The soot is just a temperature indicator. The process will take the metal back to a dead-soft condition."

HAMMER ON

Though he starts the actual shaping with a plastic mallet, stretching the metal through the center, Bruce realizes right away that the creation of this fender will require a lot of shrinking as well. "Those little hand shrinkers are almost essential, they're really handy. You could make the piece with mostly stretching, but it's really a lot of hammering, a lot more work that way."

To eliminate most of the lumps left from the plastic mallet, Bruce uses a slap hammer and a post dolly and then moves to the English wheel.

"With the wheel, you have to understand the tracking, note the pattern. As I work the panel I

continued, page 103

I modified the bending jig (seen on page 98) which is used as an aid in forming the many curved cross section pieces or ribs.

After bending I check the ribs against a line drawing made on the fabrications table.

Now the cross section braces are coming along nicely.

Now the backside of the ribs are welded from behind for strength and to be out of the way of the outer surface.

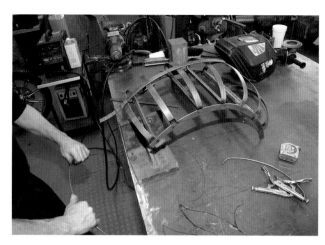

There she sits. The main frame of the buck is taking shape.

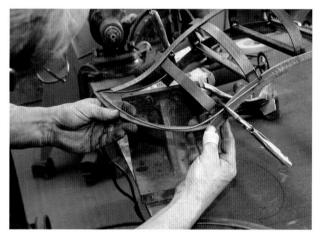

Now I shape the trail area using round rod to assist in achieving a smooth shape.

Here the tail section of the buck is formed and welded in place with a short shape-support indicator.

I'm using a flat piece of art paper which I pie-cut so it will fit the buck.

This helps us in determining the size of aluminum sheet needed.

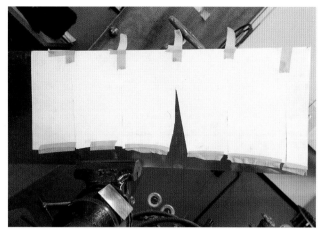

It is always best to go a little large when you cut out the actual raw panel.

Time to anneal the sheet aluminum. I am using a dusting of acetylene smoke as a guide to the proper annealing temperature.

Darn. That doesn't fit very well.

Well, I need to hammer this H14 with a Teflon hammer in order to start the stretching process.

Focusing on the crown of the fender I continue to hammer – thus stretching the annealed material.

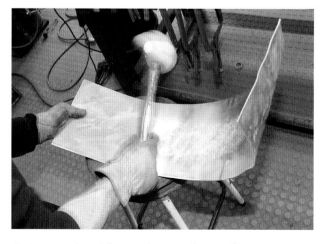

It is scary, but I know the stretching is happening.

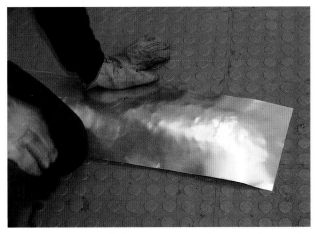

Holding the panel flat you can see how much stretching has been achieved so far.

Let's keep going on the ends.

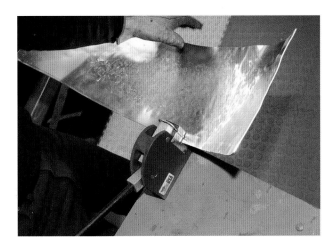

One way to speed up the process is to shrink down the edges with this economic and common shrinker tool.

Next I smooth some of the bumps out with a lightweight slapping hammer I purchase from Ron Covell.

I keep checking to be sure we are heading in the right direction with our shape.

A little wheel work will smooth out the lumps and add to the stretching.

Now that I have the general shape I'm going to run this panel through the English wheel. The lines indicate a typical wheeling pattern.

The wheel smoothes things out nicely.

Let's see if we can get it even smoother.

I can also use this wheel to apply pressure, thus raising or stretching the panel into shape.

never stop in the same place twice and then after running it through the wheel I turn the metal 90 degrees and go through the same process.

Time for a test fit, "at this point I have pretty good contact on center part of the ribs but not at the outer edges."

SHRINKING AND WHEELING

The next step is back to the shrinker, "what really accelerates the speed of the overall shaping is the shrinking," explains Bruce. "The wheel is nice because it makes the aluminum shiny so you can see what you're doing.

At this point we have good shape at the front and less shape farther back on the panel. Along

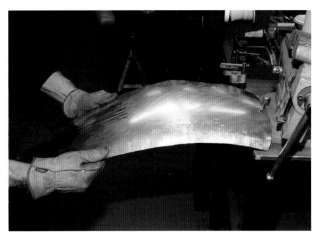

Time now to look at this panel and get a general feel for how it is progressing.

Look at all that shape that we have established.

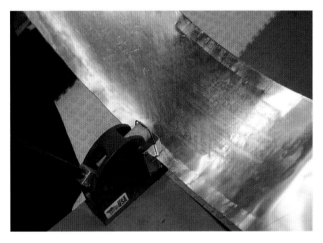

A little more shrinking along the edges will bring our panel into shape.

Let's check our shape with one of these cool shape transfer tools. The fender has a ways to go.

Once again, back on the buck to check for fit.

And then back to the shrinker.

the way Bruce does frequent test fits. At this point the center part of the fender is fitting better, though the tail needs to be stretched because it flares out,

As is common with most of these fabrication projects, the shape evolves slowly. To ensure he puts the fender on the buck in the same position each time Bruce drills a hole and inserts a spring loaded Cleco.

With a combination of the English wheel and the small shrinker, Bruce creates more crown in the back of the fender in the center, I've marked the area with a marker. I'm' going to put it back on the wheel."

One of the hardest areas to shape is the tail, as Bruce explains, "this area is tough because it's an inverse compound curve." And for a really hard area like this Bruce brings out one of the oldest metal shaping tools around, the hollowed-out tree stump, explaining, "that stump has exactly the shape I want."

Hammering the fender over the stump is interspersed with more shrinker work and more time spent working the fender on the post dolly with a slapper.

Now it's time for more shrinker work and another test fit. "When I use the shrinker I always take a full depth shrink and then go back and take a half depth shrink." About this time Bruce decides that what he needs is "more flip at the end. Like I said, that tail is a very hard shape to create."

"Once you have a little experience you can gauge the progress by carefully looking over the piece and with your hand. The contour gauge (seen on page 104) is another good way to check the progress of the shape against the buck."

"You can move metal faster with a hammer, than the wheel," explains Bruce, "so I'm going to raise metal at the transition area and then smooth it out with the post dolly and then do another test fit."

continued, page 112

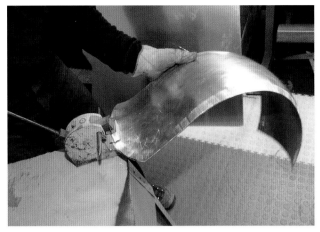

This tail section is a reverse compound shape. I need to stretch the bottom edge.

Yet again I will test the fit.

Looking good clamped in place.

Here I am using the wheel to help flip the tail section.

Yet some more shrinking.

A short study to understand the movement of this complex shape change.

Here I'm still focusing on the tail section.

Using these cool post dollies from Canada I continue to shape to tail.

The inverse compound shape is the toughest of all. Time to go to the Ol' tree stump.

Looks like we have a long way to go.

25 years ago I took a chainsaw to a stump to form this inverse curve.

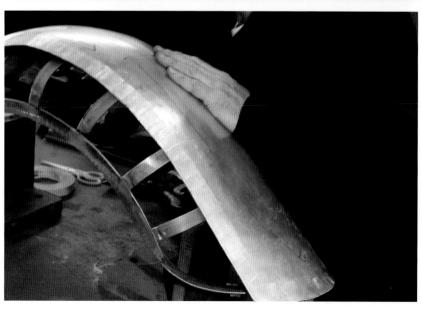

Once again back to the buck.

Pulling the radius around again with the shrinking tool.

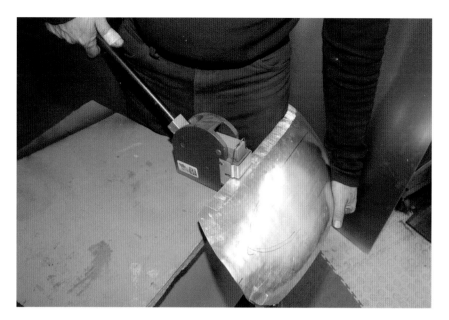

This is feeling good now. The aluminum is getting smooth and shiny.

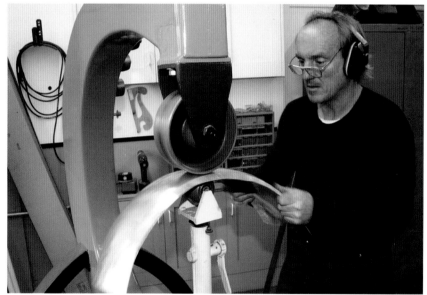

Thank goodness for the Ol' inverse curve stump tool.

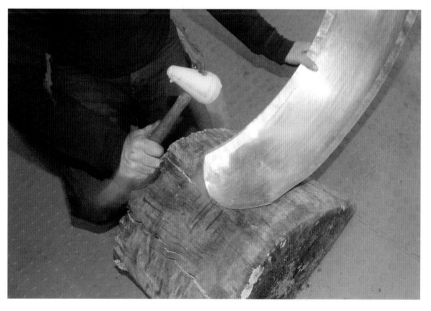

Looking under the buck I can see I have a long way to go.

Here I'm using the wheel to stretch and raise the panel.

It's raising and getting smoother with every pass.

Let's check the cross section again with our handy curve gauge.

A few more stretching blows with a broader Teflon hammer.

Looks like that tail is holding our panel up from seating on the buck.

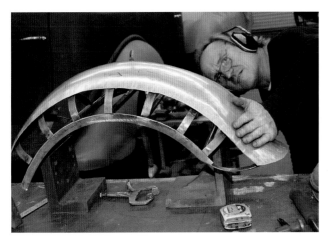

I can see now what I need to do. I need to raise the part under my hand and flip the tail farther.

Yet more slapping with the "Covell Slapper".

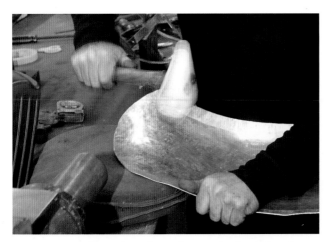

I'm moving the tail outbound over the lead shot bag.

And back to the post dolly for more refinements.

This is the part of the project where it's a great deal of making small changes, checking, and then making additional small changes. The changes are often so subtle that they are hard to discern especially for the camera.

Bruce anneals the end of the fender again (not shown) "otherwise the metal will work harden and then it will split." After annealing it's back to the post dolly. The slap hammer is a great tool you can actually move the metal in a certain direction with e direction of your blows.

On page 115 you can see the "finished fender" and though there's still work to do our deadline requires this stopping point. Despite the fact that the fender isn't quite done, we have shown a variety of shaping methods, as well as the creation and use of a buck as a fabricating aid.

Captions by Bruce Terry

That fit is looking pretty good.

Now, about that tail area…….

…a bit more slapping to flair the tail edge.

The tail really flairs out at the bottom.

Now, that's more like it.

A bit more shaping on the stump.

INTERVIEW, BRUCE TERRY

Bruce, give us a little background, how long have you been a fabricator and how did you get started?

I've had my own fabricating business for about 20 years,

It started when I was working on vintage cars, basically when I get good at one thing I get bored. It got to the point where painting bored me. I always get intrigued by things I don't know how to do. So I started doing patch panels, learning how to butt weld them in place. Pretty soon the panels got bigger and bigger and as they got bigger they had to have some shape.

There was no one in those days to teach you, you just had to work on the metal to make it fit the space. Pretty soon I gave up the body shop and went to work for Thomas Kreed, that was strictly metal work. I went from the top of one profession to the bottom of the other.

It was a sacrifice, you have to have the passion to do this. There's a big learning curve in metal shaping. That's what I love, you never know it all. There's always a new challenge, that's the beauty of it. The exciting part is getting involved in projects that need creativity, hot rods and custom bikes and that kind of thing, so you mix creativity and the craft. I always say, 'there are people who are good craftsmen. Very few are really good artists.'

Tell us a little about the tools someone at home needs to do basic metal shaping?

To be reasonable, they need what we used. A good hammer and dolly set. With aluminum you can use carved hardwood, Grind the wood to the shape you want and beat the metal over that. You also need a leather hammer and some wood mallets and assorted T- dollies. The little shrinker-stretchers are pretty much critical, especially for the price. You don't need a break, you can bend it by hand with a hammer working over an edge.

For welding you should start with an oxy-acetylene torch, for a home shop that's the most bang for the buck. Learn how to weld with that. It also makes a softer weld for aluminum than a TIG does. A small MIG is nice if you have the money. You can have all that stuff for one thousand to fifteen hundred dollars.

The three tools you really need are patience, practice and persistence.

Any tips on learning the craft?

The books are good to help people understand the concepts. But you have to really be hands-on to learn to do something with the metal. Take a piece of metal and start shaping it. You need to understand the principles, the shrinking and stretching. You have to understand what's going on. Everything is just shrinking and stretching and breaking (bending). That's all there is. I'm self-taught. I beat on the metal until I learned how to make shapes. Everybody should start out forming parts by hand. To get a feel for it, 400 years ago they were doing swords and armor by hand.

What about materials, how do you decide whether to use steel or aluminum?

Well, shaping steel takes more energy, it's not as malleable. If it's a part that gets vibration you want steel. It's not that much harder to shape, especially if you get aluminum-killed steel. You need to apply the same techniques to steel as aluminum. Steel is generally more durable, and for most people it's easier to weld steel. If you learn oxy-acetylene welding and get good at planishing, that's a good skill. I would start on steel.

Why do people fail?

You have to be willing to invest the time, you have to pay your dues, it seems like people don't want to pay the dues. Guys who come to my seminars are blown away by what they can accomplish. If they're driven enough they can probably learn it. Motorcycles are smaller and have more shape so in some ways the parts are easier to shape. The most difficult parts to make are the flat things, like a hood. A hood is hard, or a door skin.

What's the most common mistake?

The worst thing you can do is over shape a piece. You can always put more shape in a panel, but you don't want to take shape out, that's a hard fix. If you don't check it all the time and you go too far. You might as well just throw it out and start over. Go slow and check your parts regularly. I like to tell my students to sneak up on it.

Our fender top section is really coming into shape.

Just a bit more slapping on the post dolly.

Clamped into place and looking good. The panel fits on the buck nicely.

Chapter Eleven

Air Dam

Ron Covell Makes an Air Dam

As we've said before, stretching is easier than shrinking especially in a small shop. Ron Covell's creation, a small air dam on a chopper, doesn't actually require a great deal of either. As Ron explained, "this is a good project for a first time home builder because it doesn't involve a lot of shaping. In terms of the design, I tried to keep the angle of the top panel parallel to the fins and the bottom lined up with the bottom of the frame."

This air dam is a fairly simple project, and it can be made with fairly common tools. It makes an ideal project for learning more about sheet metal fabrication.

MATERIAL

For material, Ron chose .063 inch 3003 H14 aluminum, but it could just as easily have been made out of steel. "I like to keep the aluminum in the original condition," explained Ron, "although I will anneal the part that needs the curl on the front."

It's interesting to note that one of the first things Ron does is construct the platform seen right under the front of the frame. As he explains, "I want the air dam in line with the bottom of the frame rail, otherwise it doesn't look right. So it's convenient to be able to set it on the platform." After deciding on the design, Ron's first step in the fabrication process is to create the first side panel from light board. He starts with a piece that's too big, and lays out the exact outline with tape.

Once he has a shape he likes, Ron transfers the shape to sheet aluminum and starts cutting it out with a saber saw. "To cut sheet steel you need a fine tooth blade," explains Ron, "but for aluminum it's not as important." Some of the details areas are cut with the tin snips, and then the edge is trimmed of any burrs with a file. Ron puts a little crown in the side panel, bending it gently by hand. Once the two side panels are cut and formed, Ron tapes them to the downtubes, and now you can really see how handy it is to have the platform as a place to put the poster board that will be the template for the bottom piece of the air dam.

The actual bottom of the air dam is cut out with the band saw, then the edges are rolled, much as Rob Roehl did in Chapter Eight. Because the aluminum came in a "half-hard" condition, Ron needs to anneal the end where it will be rolled up to meet the next panel. "You can anneal only as much of the panel as you're going to work," explains Ron, "which leaves the rest of the panel in the hardened, and stronger, condition. After heating the front of the panel you can either quench the piece with water or let it air cool, the net effect is the same."

Continued page 123

We want the bottom of the air dam in line with the bottom of the frame, so a support is rigged to hold the parts in the proper alignment.

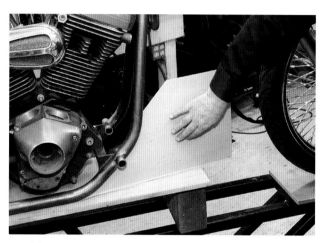

Holding a piece of chip board against the support, it is slid toward the frame and trimmed to have a good fit against the down tube.

While not essential, it's helpful to use an angle bracket to hold the pattern for the side of the air dam perfectly vertical.

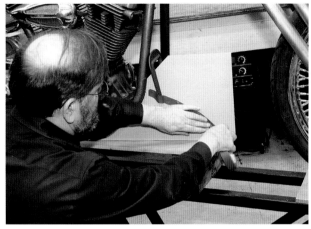

The side pattern is made oversize, and once the bottom and back edge are finalized, masking tape is used to lay out the top edge.

And here's the finished pattern for the sides of the air dam, trimmed to size. Be sure you like the shape before going on to the next step!

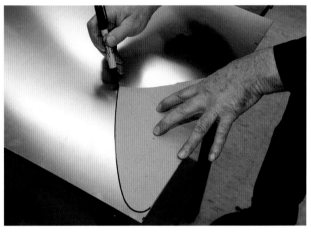

The pattern is laid on a sheet of .063" thickness 3003 H-14 Aluminum, and the edges are marked for trimming. You could use steel, as well.

Here we're using a saber saw to cut on the line.

Tight radius cuts are easier to manage with aircraft shears than a saber saw, but these shears work best for trimming edges, not for cutting pieces from a sheet.

Always deburr the edges of freshly-cut panels, to avoid cuts on your hands.

We're curving the panel a little more by holding one end against the workbench, and pulling the other end.

Here we're bringing the curve closer to the rear of the panel.

Although the sides of the air dam could be flat, we thought they'd look better with a little curve to them. Here you can see the slight curve added so far.

Now we're trying both sides in place on the support structure. We can get a better feel for the proportions of the air dam.

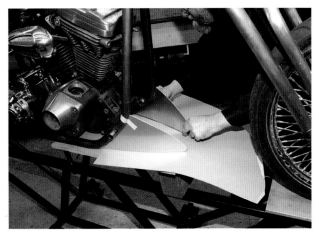

Since we're happy with the size, shape, and curve of the air dam sides, we'll use them to make the pattern for the bottom.

We're using tape to hold the air dam sides centered on the frame tubes, and now we can draw against the sides to mark the bottom pattern.

And here's the bottom pattern. Notice that we chose to give the air dam a slight peak in the center, for a little extra style.

We're using a bandsaw to cut the base to size, but a saber saw would work just as well, although it cuts a little more slowly.

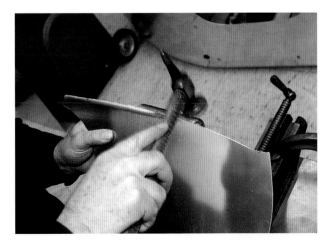

The bottom plate is basically flat, but the edges are curled to 45 degrees. We're using a T dolly to curl the edges.

The edges are held slightly above the T dolly, and tapped with a body hammer to create the curl.

One edge is curled here – this only takes a few minutes to accomplish. Go slowly, and work toward getting the curl consistent from end to end.

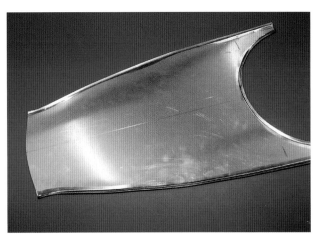

Here both sides and the back edge are curled. We decided to anneal, or soften, the aluminum to make the large curl on the front edge easier to form.

Annealing is a two-step process. The first step is to put a light coating of soot on the metal from a pure acetylene flame.

Next, a neutral flame is used to heat the metal until the soot just barely burns off. Be very careful not to overheat the metal, or it will melt!

Here the soot is burned completely off in the area where the large curl goes.

We're quenching the metal with water so we can handle it without waiting for it to cool. The metal will be softened even if we don't quench it.

We're working over the T dolly again to create the front curl. We're using a 'slap hammer' which has a larger face than a body hammer.

Notice that the ends of the T dolly are rounded, allowing them to fit into the radiused corners of the part.

This curl is larger than the previous ones, so it takes a little more hammering.

The curl is worked slowly and evenly, gradually going across the part from one side to the other.

The part is continually moved on the T dolly to bring it into the most advantageous position.

Again, the ball-shaped end of the T dolly is used where the two radiused edges meet.

3. This is the easiest time to build the mounts. We're making two simple brackets that will weld to the frame, allowing screws to support the bottom of the air dam.

As shown in the photos, the actual shaping at the nose of the bottom panel is done with a slapper, working over a T-dolly. Once the side and bottom panels are formed, Ron sets them in place and designs a set of brackets. As he explains, "this is the time to make and attach brackets, while we can still get at the down-tubes."

Next, Ron adds some curl or crown to the edge or lip of the side panel. Again, this is similar to what Rob did with the air cleaner cover. Ron has a variety of tools in his shop, he shows us first how to roll the edges of the side panels by hand working over a T-Dolly, and then by running the edges through a set or rounding-over dies.

Continued page 127

1. After curling the front edge, the panel was no longer flat, so a clamp is being used here to pull the center down, regaining the flatness.

2. Here we're checking the fit of the first two panels. They fit very well!

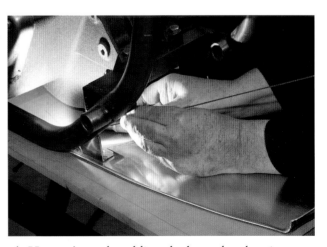

4. Here we're tack welding the lower brackets into place while our access is still unimpeded.

1. These tools are called transfer punches. They are used to mark the center for holes to be drilled.

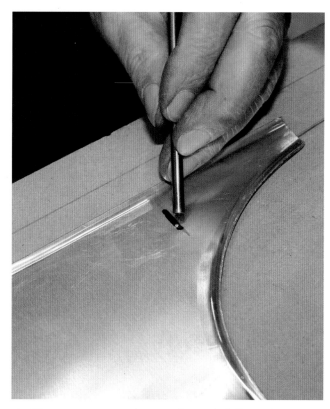

3. Here you can see the punch mark left on the aluminum.

2. With the bottom panel in place, the transfer punch is put through the hole in the bracket, and tapped to mark the center for the mounting hole.

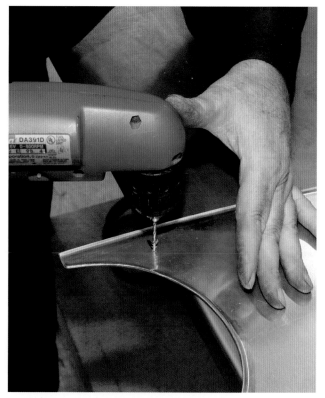

4. With the center accurately marked, it's easy to drill the mounting holes with an electric drill. We are using #10 screws for mounting.

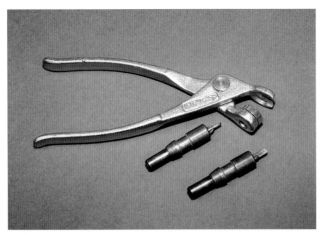

These are Clecos, and Cleco pliers. They are like an easily removable rivet, and they're great for holding parts together temporarily.

The Cleco pliers are put on the Cleco and squeezed, then the tip is inserted into the holes.

When the pliers are released, the Cleco holds the parts tightly together.

Now we'll look at the fit of the right-side panel for the air dam, and examine how well it fits against the base.

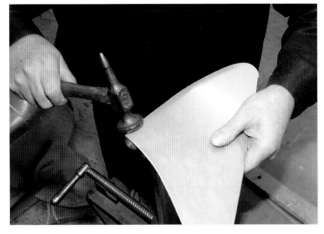

Everything seems to be in order, so we'll start curling the edges of the side piece, again working over a T-dolly.

Again, the rounded nose of the T dolly is ideal for getting into tightly-radiused corners.

There are machines that can speed the process of curling edges. This is a beading machine, with 'rounding over' dies installed.

If you look closely, you'll see the top die has a flange, and the bottom die has a matching groove – these work together to roll the curl on the panel's edge.

The rounding-over dies are available in various dimensions and are sometimes used one after the other to create a particular radius.

The rounding-over dies make fast work of rolling a curl on straight or slightly curved edges.

For tightly-radiused curves, like the front of this panel, the T-dolly is still the best tool to use.

THE WELDING

With all the parts fitting together pretty well and all the matching edges crowned, Ron begins tack welding. During this process Ron uses spring-loaded Clecos to hold the bottom panel in place, obviously you could use small bolts or whatever is handy in your shop.

Though some of the later welding is done with the gas welder, the tack welding and the seams done at this stage are all done with the TIG welder using 1100 rod. Ron explains that aluminum requires more heat than steel, because the heat is conducted through the material so fast. For this job he recommends a welder with a minimum output of 80 amps that can work in AC mode. "I seamed the inside of the seam, with no filler rod, it makes for a better looking seam and it also makes for a stronger weld, in case there's a spot where I didn't get good penetration on the outside bead for example."

The top panel is mocked up, cut and shaped last. As you can see the partially finished assembly is bolted to the downtubes and then a piece of board is cut to size and used as a template to cut out the panel. To give the top panel some character Ron starts bending it by hand, then gives it a bit of crown with the English wheel.

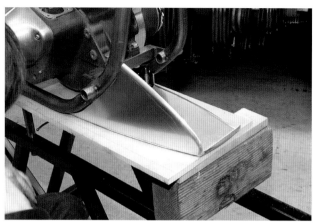

With all the edges curled, we'll check the fit of the panels again. Everything looks great, so we're ready to tack weld the panels together.

We're using a TIG welder here. We'll demonstrate oxy-acetylene welding later.

We're using masking tape to temporarily hold the panels into position for tack welding.

In preparation for welding, we're closely checking the fit between the panels one more time.

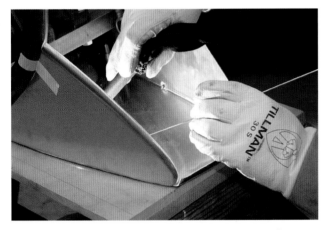

Now we're tacking the second side panel onto the base. The tacks are made on the inside simply because the access is better there.

Here we're using a belt sander to sharpen the tungsten electrode for the TIG welder.

With a few tacks on the inside holding the parts together, the assembly is put on the bench so that more tacks can be put on the outside.

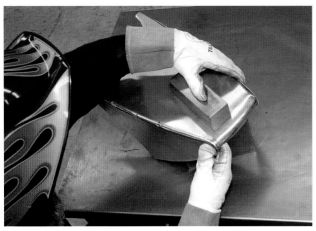

We're using a support underneath, and a weight on top, to hold the assembly in a convenient position for adding more tack welds.

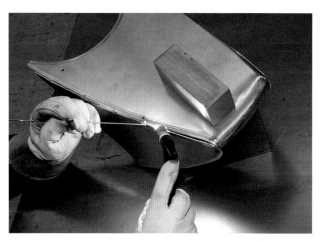

We want our tack welds to be no more than 1 inch apart.

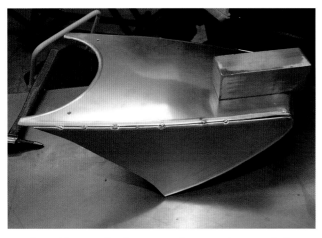

Tack welding is fairly easy as long as the panels fit well together. Any gaps at the joint would make the tack welding much more difficult.

The fit at the tip of the side panels needs a little trimming, so we're using the aircraft shears to adjust the fit accordingly.

A little tapping is sometimes required to close any gaps at the joint before tack welding.

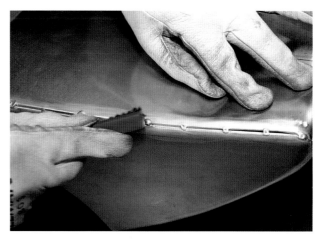

Now that we have the tacks properly positioned, the joint is cleaned with a stainless steel brush in preparation for the finish welding.

Covell: Gas Welding Aluminum

The trick to gas welding aluminum is practice. There is carry over from welding steel, yet aluminum is unique. You have to modify your technique to accommodate aluminum. The only way to get onto that is through practice. Regarding the size of the tip, the orifice should be 2/3 of the thickness of the metal being welding." Some say you should use low pressure on the regulator, but I don't.

Regardless of what regulators are set at, I have all the control I need with the valves on

Note the pressures, higher than what is normally recommended, yet Ron was able to adjust the flame at the torch.

the torch itself. I use a minimum of 3 psi of acetylene and 5 psi of oxygen. Today I have 15 psi of acetylene and 20 of oxygen, that's what I used yesterday with that big rose-bud torch, and I'm using the same regulator settings today for the aluminum. I know this will work and I can make all my adjustments at the torch.

It's important to scrub the seam before you start welding, it does two things. First, it cleans the joint, of course. Second, it also leaves a rough surface that the flux sticks to more easily. You don't need a lot of flux, just a thin coat. When the flux is heated it gives off a gaseous shield that excludes atmospheric oxygen from the weld zone.

Local welding stores don't have the aluminum-welding flux, odds on finding it at the same place you buy your welding rods are slim to none. I buy it either from Fournier Enterprises or TM technologies (see Sources). In certain places the water seems to contaminate the flux so I always use bottled water. The flux gives off an intense yellow glare, which is why you need a special lens in your welding goggles for gas welding aluminum.

One of the reasons people find gas welding aluminum difficult is that their experience is based on welding steel. When steel gets hot to melting it glows red so you can judge the temperature by the color of metal.

With aluminum there is no color change, the material is the same light grey color at room temperature as it is when it melts onto the floor. So the signs the you have a puddle when welding aluminum are more subtle.

Once you know what to look for you

Covell: Gas Welding Aluminum

can see when you have a puddle, but it takes experience to recognize that. Another difference between the two is the torch angle. With steel the angle is 60 to 45 degrees between the torch and the work. With aluminum it more like 30 degrees. The torch is much flatter when welding aluminum. If you hold it too upright the pressure of the flame can actually blow a hole in the metal.

I weld right to left because I'm right handed. It's not good practice to start welding at the edge of the metal and go to the end. A crack may form if you start at the edge. So what I do is start an inch from the edge and then weld to the edge. Then I stop for a moment and complete the weld. Having support for my body is real important too, so I lean on the table.

When you are finished welding it's important that the flux be washed off soon. The material is caustic or corrosive and if left in place more than a few hours it starts to corrode the aluminum. Fortunately it's water soluble and washes off easily."

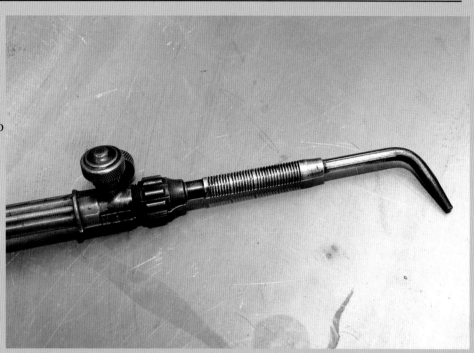

The size of the tip is relative to the size gauge or thickness of the metal, Ron recommends 2/3 the thickness of the metal as the orifice size.

Gas welding aluminum requires a smaller angle between the torch and the metal, so the flame is less likely to blow through the panel. Yellow glare means you need a special lens for the welding goggles.

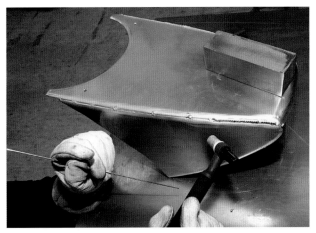

Now we're starting the finish weld with the TIG torch. The filler rod is 1100 alloy, 1/16" diameter.

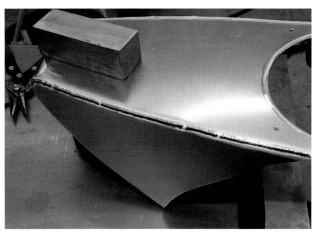

And here's the second seam, finish welded. Notice the consistency of the width and height of the weld bead – this comes with practice!

On parts where the appearance of the inside is important, we'll often make a second welding pass on the inside, fusing the metal together without adding any rod.

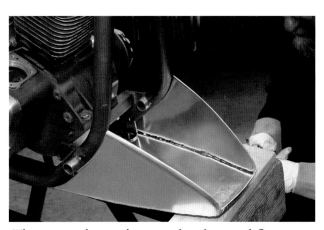

This optional second pass makes the metal flow together more neatly on the inside.

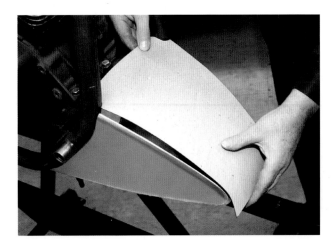

Now we're ready to make a chip board pattern for the top piece.

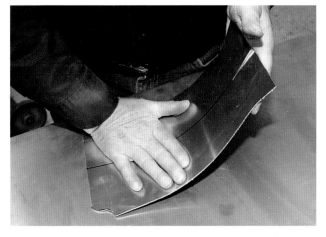

We're giving the piece a gentle curve by holding one edge against the workbench, and lifting the other end.

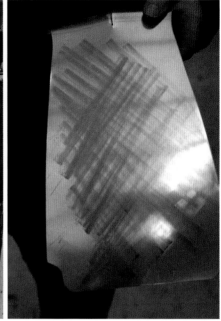

Using the T-dolly again, the front edge of the top piece is curled.

This machine is an English wheel. We're using it to give a domed surface to the top of the air dam. This can be done with hand tools, too.

The lines on the metal were left by the contact points where the wheels touched the metal. Notice the two directions of wheeling so far.

THE WHEEL

As Ron explains, "the English wheel creates compound curves. It creates curvature north to south and east to west at the same time. This is essentially a stretching operation, the pressure between the wheels stretches the metal. When I select a wheel I chose the lower wheel with the contour closest to what I'm trying to achieve."

Ron runs the first series of passes at an angle that's diagonal to the length of the panel. Then he runs another series of passes through the wheel that are at 90 degrees to the first series of passes, explaining as he does, "the most important thing is to cross the tracks, as it gets out the little low spots, it's like the pattern people use when they block sand." After Ron has enough crown in the metal he puts a crease down the center with nothing more sophisticated than a hammer and a dull chisel, explaining as he does, "I want to add a body line in the panel to match the body line in the top of the gas tank."

FITMENT

As always, fitment of the panels is critical and Ron makes sure the new top panel fits the other three as perfectly as possible. Anything larger then a very small gap means more heat, more filler rod and the resulting change in dimension. "Sometimes with beginners one of the hardest things is learning how to fix all the little spots where two pieces don't quite fit," explains Ron. "But with time and experience it's pretty easy, though at first that part can be really hard."

Some people think you can only weld aluminum with a TIG welder, but that is not the case. In fact there are some advantages to gas welding the aluminum. Though the seam might not be quite as pretty, it's much more workable or malleable. Check out the side-bar in this chapter for more on gas welding aluminum.

continued page 140

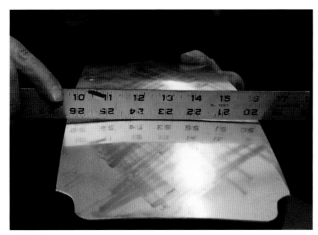

Here we're holding a straightedge against the part, so you can see the right-to-left curve the English wheel put into the panel.

Now we're wheeling some more, in a new direction, to smooth the panel.

In this shot, you'll see that the top wheel is flat, and the lower wheel has a gradual radius. There is a narrow flat spot in the center of the lower wheel.

Most English wheels come with a set of wheels, each with a different radius. This machine has a set of 6 wheels – a nice assortment!

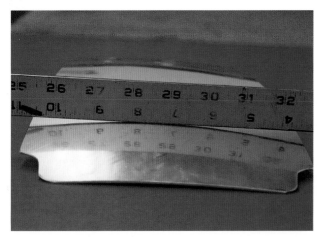

After just a few minutes of wheeling, the part has taken on a nicely domed shape, and is fairly smooth. Again, this comes with practice.

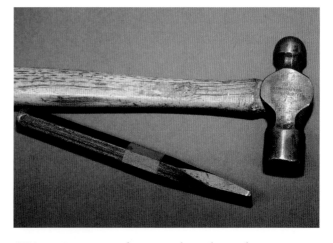

We're going to use these simple tools – a hammer, and a chisel with a blunted tip, to put a ridge down the center of the air dam.

We've drawn a center line inside the top panel, and using a sandbag for support, the chisel is tapped lightly with the hammer, working down the line.

A chisel and hammer, and some discretion, are used to put a body line in the top of the air dam.

With one light round of hammering, a very noticeable ridge has been formed.

With a couple more rounds of hammering, the ridge is much more pronounced. We could go farther, but we're satisfied with the look at this point.

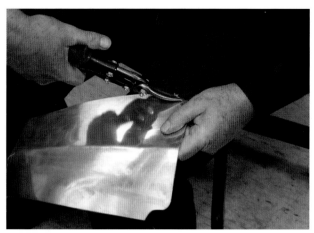

We're into the home stretch, now. The top edges of the panel are notched with aircraft shears where they fit against the down tubes of the frame.

Although we could use a T dolly to curl the edges, the rounding-over dies are faster and more consistent.

The top panel is tried into place to check the fit with the side panels.

The front edge needs a little more curl, so we'll go back to the T dolly and tap it a bit.

The tightly-radiused corner need a little tune-up against the rounded end of the T-dolly.

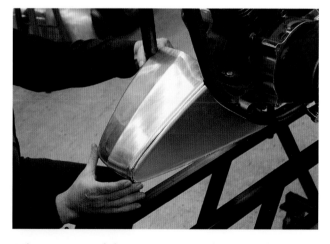

The contours of the parts are matching nearly perfectly, but there is a little overlap at the front edge.

The panel is trimmed with aircraft shears in preparation for tack welding.

The front edge of the base has a slight wave, which is fixed with a few well-placed taps with a body hammer.

Here the parts have been tack-welded together with the TIG. We're going to demonstrate gas welding for this seam.

Flux is required to gas weld aluminum. The flux comes as a powder, which is mixed with water to make a light paste.

We like to use bottled water to ensure that no impurities contaminate the flux.

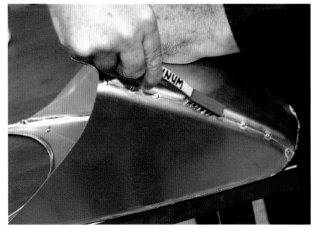

Cleanliness is essential for gas welding aluminum, so use a stainless brush to clean the joint before applying the flux.

The flux is applied to both sides of the joint with the type of brush used for spreading acid when soldering.

A special lens is needed for gas welding aluminum, too. This lens is made by the Cobra company, and it completely cuts the glare given off by the flux.

A thin coating of flux is all that's needed. We like to mix our flux in a disposable container. It doesn't keep well after mixing, we discard it at the end of the day.

As you can see, the flux gives off an intensely bright orange glare when heated – that's why the special lens is necessary.

Gas welding aluminum is a little tricky, and takes a lot of practice! Notice that the torch is laid down fairly flat.

As soon as a puddle forms, the rod is dipped, quickly withdrawn, and the torch is advanced a bit more. Once you get the rhythm, it seems to work best when you move along quickly.

We're not getting much distortion on this air dam, since all the joints have a curl, which strengthens the edges. Flat panels warp the worst!

And here's the finished weld – fairly uniform in both width and height.

It's important to wash the flux off quickly – don't let it set overnight, or you'll get corrosion. Now we'll file the welds smooth.

The 'Vixen' files preferred for this have very coarse, curved teeth, but they leave a fairly smooth surface.

The file will reveal any low spots on the panel too, so we generally file the entire piece, and tap up any low spots that are revealed.

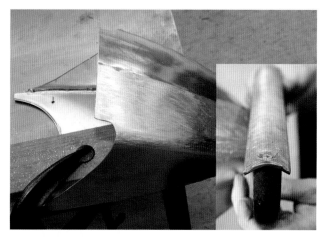

The area near the peak is slightly concave, so a curved Vixen file must be used in this area.

We're using the sander to carefully knock down the weld on the leading edge of the air dam.

A sanding disk can be used to cut the weld down. It's faster, but can make thin spots - so be very careful.

FINISH WORK

A vixen file is Ron's tool of choice to the finishing work. "Because I was careful when I shaped the parts," explains Ron, "I didn't find any low spots. If I hadn't been so careful I would find low spots that would have to be tapped up with a hammer." There are actually two (at least) vixen files in Ron's tool box. The second is convex which makes it easier to get at the concave part of the upper panel. "People should know that you don't have to metal finish every high and low spot out of the metal," says Ron. "Use of filler is perfectly acceptable as long as you understand the limitations. I like the craftsmanship of the metal finishing, knowing that there's no filler, or very little filler needed before painting a piece."

When Ron finishes the finishing with a grinder equipped with an 80 grit pad, as shown nearby. As Ron explains, "the sander isn't as esoteric as a file but it gets the job done. How far you take the metal finishing is up to you."

Captions by Ron Covell

Here we're using an angle plate to hold the air dam securely in the upside-down position, so we can power sand the bottom welds.

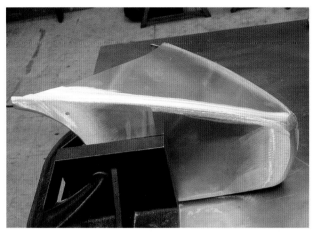

Although you can't get panels quite as smooth by power-sanding as you can by filing, we got a pretty decent blending of contours on this part.

Here we're using a 3" diameter right-angle sander to carefully work down the weld on the tightly-radiused corner. It would be pretty easy to sand the metal thin with the big sander here!

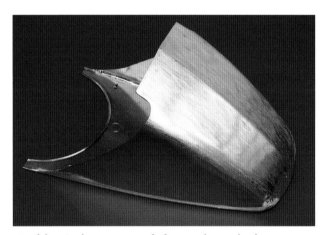

And here's the part, sanded smooth on the bottom portion, and filed smooth on the top.

Checking the fit on the bike, we can see that it has come out just as we planned.

So with just a few hours work, you can make a pretty cool air dam for your bike! Don't be afraid – just dive right in and have some fun!

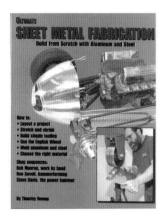

ULTIMATE SHEET METAL FABRICATION

From how-to author Tim Remus comes Ultimate Sheet Metal Fabrication. Intended to answer the needs of hot rod, motorcycle and aircraft enthusiasts, this book is primarily a series of hands-on fabrication sequences.

Well known expert Ron Covell shows how to shape a panel over a hammerform while Steve Davis creates a deck lid with the power hammer. Bob

Munroe makes his motorcycle fender using the English wheel with help from a hammer working over a bag of sand. Additional sequences include everything from a simple blower scoop to the fabrication of an automobile fender. Though hands-on sequences make up most of this book, the first three chapters cover Planning & Design, Mock-up and Material choice, and Sheet Metal Welding.

Eleven Chapters	144 Pages	$19.95	Over 300 photos-100% color

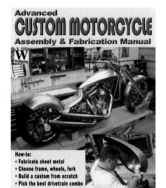

ADV CUSTOM MOTORCYCLE ASSEMBLY & FABRICATION

What started in the mid-90s when a few people decided to build "stock Softails" from aftermarket parts – because they couldn't buy one at the dealer – has evolved into a full blown industry. Today, every small town has a Chopper or Custom bike shop and every cable TV channel has a Biker-Build-Off series. No longer content to build copies of stock motorcycles, today's builder wants a motorcycle that's longer,

lower and sexier than anything approved by a factory design team.

Part catalog, part service manual and part inspiration, this new book offers help with Planning the project, getting the right look and actually assembling that custom bike you've dreamed about for years.

Nine Chapters	144 Pages	$24.95	Over 400 photos-100% color

HOW TO HOP-UP AND CUSTOMIZE YOUR HARLEY-DAVIDSON BAGGER

Baggers don't have to be slow and they don't have to look like every other Dresser in the parking lot. Take your Bagger from slow to show with a few more cubic inches, a little paint and some well placed accessories.

Written by well-known author Tim Remus, this book shows you how to upgrade the engine, lower the bike, and personalize the paint and sheet metal. Images help explain exactly what it takes to install a

set of springs in the front forks or re-program the fuel injection map. Follow along as the project bike, a 2004 Standard, makes the transition from stock to custom: including an upgrade to 95 cubic inches and the addition of a flamed paint job laid out over the standard black urethane.

Whether you're looking for additional power or more visual pizazz, the answers and ideas you need are contained in this great book.

Eight Chapters	144 Pages	$24.95	400+ color images - 100% color

TRIUMPH MOTORCYCLE RESTORATION

As popular as the Triumph Twins were in the 60s and 70s, they are quite possibly more popular now. The new book from Wolfgang Publications offers complete start-to-finish assembly and restoration sequences on two Triumph Twins, a 1963 Bonneville and a 1969 Bonneville. Also included is the start-to-finish assembly of the 1969 engine and transmission. Rather than try to describe the minis-

cule differences that often separated one year from another, this book offers a color gallery with left and right side views of all significant models from 1959 to 1970. With over 450 color photos, Triumph Restoration offers 144 pages of hard-core how-to help for anyone who wants to repair or restore their own Triumph twin.

Eight Chapters	144 Pages	$29.95	Over 200 color images

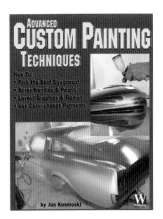

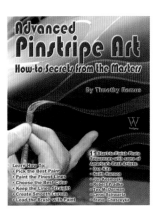
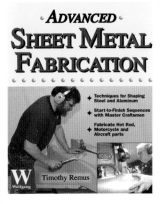

Sources

Cap Technology/Dagger Tools
47757 West Road, Unit C-106
Wixom, MI 48393
Craig Peterson
248-735-1123
www.daggertools.com

Covell Creative Metalworking
106 Airport Boulevard, #105
Freedom, CA 95019
Toll Free 800-747-4631
www.covell.biz

D&D – FatKatz
140 E. Mcknight Way #2
Grass Valley, CA 95945
530-273-2212
Toll Free Order Line: 877-432-8528
www.fatkatz.com

Fournier Enterpirsies
800-501-3722
www.furnierenterprises.com

Mississippi Welders Supply
www.mwsco.com
Hudson store:
1810 Webster St.
Hudson, WI 54016

Rob Roehl
c/o Donnie Smith Custom Cycles
10594 Raddison Rd NE
Blaine, MN 55449

Bruce Terry
Specialty Metal Fabrication
517 Airport Way
Unit M
Monterey, CA 93940
www.specialtymetalfabrication.com

TM Technologies
tinmantech.com
530-292-3506

SPD Specialty Product Design
11252 Sunco Drive
Ranch Cordova, CA 95742
888-778-3312
www.spdexhaust.com

Russ Wernimont (RWD)
37100 Applegate Road
Murrieta, CA 92563
951-698-9495
951-461-7066
www.russwernimont.com

www.metalshapers.org